To Dear Brown Johnny,
    Wife Dottie & their
"growing" family —
With fond & happy
memories of our growing
up years together.
May the links pour magic
in your life.
            Much Love,
                Beth

A HERITAGE OF HERBS

A HERITAGE
OF HERBS

Bertha P. Reppert

Illustrated by Margaret S. Browne
and Marjorie L. Reppert

Stackpole Books

A HERITAGE OF HERBS

Published by
STACKPOLE BOOKS
Cameron and Kelker Streets
Harrisburg, Pa. 17105

Published simultaneously in Don Mills, Ontario, Canada
by Thomas Nelson & Sons, Ltd.

Printed in the U.S.A.

Library of Congress Cataloging in Publication Data
Reppert, Bertha P.
  A heritage of herbs.

  Bibliography: p.
  Includes index.
  1 Herb gardening. 2. Gardens—United States—
History. 3. Herbs. 4. Cookery (Herbs) I. Title.
SB351.H5R44   635'.7'0973   76-8239
ISBN 0-8117-0796-2

To my husband, Byron,
Who makes all things possible;
and
To our daughters,
Carolynn, Marjorie, Nancy, and Susanna,
For whom this rich Heritage of Herbs
Is a rightful legacy

An
Early
American
Society
Book

The editors of *Early American Life,* the Society's official magazine, have checked this book for historical and, where possible, factual accuracy. Opinions and interpretations expressed within its pages have been left as written by the author. It is the objective of the Society to sponsor and recommend books that it feels have lasting value to persons interested in colonial and early American times—books that are both entertaining and enlightening.

Robert G. Miner
President and Editor of Publications

Contents

Acknowledgments

IT IS FITTING to express my gratitude to all who have encouraged me in the writing of this book, those whom I know personally and those I have not met except through their own written words. Surely everyone concerned is encompassed in this blanket of thanks.

My debt to my long-suffering family is enormous. They have indulged me to the limit and I acknowledge their patience, their never-ceasing help and endurance, all with great love. This hobby is not always easy to live with when it takes over house (cellar to attic) and time (twelve months of the year) and property in two locations. They have somehow managed to live with all that — and me.

The endless encouragement and confidence of my sister Hildegard is awesome, to be cherished and treasured forever. And dear friend Teresa Kuentz, who shared all my enthusiasms — how do I thank her? Bouquets of rosemary both to sister and to friend!

All my beloved garden club friends have contributed to this

work over the many years during which our mutual love for the same remarkable source of life has proven a strong bond of inspiration and learning.

A special thank you to Marty Crawford and Margaret Browne, fellow Rosemarians, who tended our Rosemary House during the long summer through while I typed and wrote and typed again. To Margaret for her garden sketches and daughter Marjorie for her line drawings of the herbs, we are especially grateful.

More thanks to Pat Humphries, who taught me to appreciate a good quotation and for sharing her secrets of propagating the noble bay, as well as for countless other collaborations over the years of our friendship; to our local library staff, especially Ellen Page, for their untiring assistance; to Quentin Schleider, friend and teacher, who took the time to send me much information on public gardens; and to all those persons across the country who responded to my queries on herb gardens to visit.

A nosegay of thanks to the multitalented Frances Mustard, who insisted that I go to Flower Show School once long ago and has shared her considerable knowledge on dyeing with plants by correcting that chapter for me; to Mrs. W. W. Clarke for her information on the honey bee; and Gladys Black and Julie Neals for their help on gardening in the South; to D. D. Dillon for permission to use the springerle cookie recipe and to Jean Gordon for permission to use her rose water recipe; to Marty Weber for much valuable source material on old-fashioned roses; to Sue Ritter, who contributed her expertise with boxwood. A "tussie-mussie" for Jeanette Coote, my 18th-century friend, for her help with the public gardens; and *donka schay* to Paul Wieand, who shared his rich heritage of Pennsylvania Dutch folklore most generously.

I have especially appreciated the great kindness of Mary Tozer, who has guided me gently through the intricacies of editing a book and is willing to do it again.

To all of those who have touched my life, beginning with my mother, and have shared my love of gardens and gardening, my heartfelt thanks for a lifetime of pleasure, now in turn to be shared with those who read this book. Most especially, of course, to dear Mrs. Dunlap, whose talk on herbs started all of this in the first place.

Introduction

EVERY NEED man has had since the beginning of time has been met by plants, directly or indirectly. Knowledge of this multitude of uses has been passed down through the centuries, transmitted between civilizations, cultures, continents. The herb has been the bridge. Now we are the fortunate beneficiaries of this vast legacy of herbal wisdom.

My own introduction to herbs came about fifteen years ago. After gardening for more years than I care to count, I couldn't believe that there was anything so remarkable to be had from the soil. But there they were, quietly awaiting my moment of discovery. It happened most unexpectedly. We had moved from New Jersey to Pennsylvania, transporting our extensive gardens in three advance trips. Among the plants was one pressed into my hand by a friend who said, "This is melissa; plant it in your new garden." And so, as instructed, I carried melissa with me and found a place for it near our new home, where it thrived. Every time I walked past it I would break off a tip, crush it in my hands, sniff it with much appreciation of its lemony fragrance, always murmuring, "This is melissa. How lovely!" At that time the herbs in my garden were the usual mints, chives, and parsley and, although I didn't recognize it as such, the charming melissa.

A year or so later, in January, I attended a garden club meeting in which a good friend and mentor* presented a remarkable program entitled "The Spice of Life," a discourse on herbs and spices and the ways in which they relate to our lives. Across the front of the room was a long line of tables covered with hundreds of items in which herbs and spices were the important ingredients. She ticked them off one by one. But, most astonishing to me (remember that this was in the bitterest cold of January), marching across the front edge of all the tables was an array of herbs, each fresh green sprig pinned to a white paper doiley. I had never seen anything prettier. Here was twelve-month gardening—things to be grown, indoors and out—that could be harvested in January. Incredible—and useful! In the midst of her display was pinned melissa, which my friend called lemon balm. I knew then what I had been given to bring to my new garden—an ancient sweet-smelling herb, useful, of great importance, one brought to these shores by our colonists, then with courage and hope and love carried west by the pioneers.

I could hardly wait to get home from the meeting, to rush through the house back to the sleeping garden, out into the snow. I dug down through several feet of it to where I knew so well was the melissa plant brought from our former home and made "hereditary in the new land." And there it was, bright chartreuse and puckery, the leaves lying close to the ground, waiting to be picked and crushed, smelled and enjoyed for all its lemony fragrance.

I managed to pull a piece from the frozen earth, brought it in to my window sill, bedded it in a pot of warm soft soil, and watched it come back to life in a few days. Soon I was growing mint and watercress, rooting garlic cloves, and starting basil seeds, filling my window sills, my house, and my life with herbs in every form, using them in many ways, enjoying them, delighting in them, and feeling grateful to my friend for her inspiring

---

* Mrs. Bruce Dunlap.

talk. She introduced me to a lifetime of gardening pleasure. I can only show my gratitude by introducing them to you.

My next logical move was an immediate trip to the local library where several herbals became my winter reading for that year — the most amazing garden books I have ever encountered. They became my close companions, books to marvel at, filled with ancient plants, historic and useful.

Be it fact or fancy, there's an "I didn't know that!" on every page. It's hard to resist tidbits such as "take the timber thereof [rosemary] and burn it to coales and make powder thereof, smell it oft and it shall keep thee youngly." Or an archaic recipe that calls for "four handfuls of Agrimony and as many of Scabious" never fails to tickle my fancy.

Fortunately man's dependency upon plants has been an engrossing subject for so many centuries that much of it has been written down. Old herbals yield their riches to us "for use and for delight." We marvel at the archaic usage of strewing mint to keep down bad smells and insects; then, in turn, think nothing of dropping a bunch of lemon balm down the garbage disposal or adding excess mint herbiage to the trash compactor or scattering clean-smelling lavender buds before the advancing vacuum cleaner. What a heavenly fragrance — the prudent housewife's solution to the same problems in the twentieth century! Is there so much difference between this and the ancient custom of strewing mint?

My enduring gratitude is extended to all the herbalists and their herbals, old and new, for their contributions to the body of this work. My knowledge grows — a bit heard here or read there, gleaned, retained, and absorbed into my own being, built upon a fact at a time, until it has become a part of me. Herbs are a universal knowledge; we have inherited a rich green legacy from those preceding us since the beginnings of time. To know herbs, then, is to love them.

Quotations sprinkled throughout the book are the words of the early herbalists, which can hardly be improved upon for wit and wisdom. They are taken from John Gerard, author of *The Herball or General Historie of Plants,* dated 1597; John Parkinson, whose *Theatrum Botanicum* was published in 1640; and, most frequently, the ever-popular Nicholas Culpeper, who wrote

English Herbals or The English Physician Enlarged, printed in London in 1653.

As for the medicinal references made in this herbal, it would not be possible to write of herbs and ignore their most ancient usage as man's first and foremost medicine. This was their primary purpose, mentioned in the first chapter of Genesis and countless times since.

We are here to enjoy the miracles of twentieth-century medicine because herbs were available when they were needed. No one would refute the value of today's prescription drugs and antibiotics, surgical techniques and medical advances. It is unfortunate that herbs were the tool of charlatans in the late 1800s and quackery placed them in disrepute. The truth is that they do indeed affect the body. Some are drugs; some are poisons. No self-medication should be attempted beyond the simple herbal teas that can aid the digestion, act as a sedative, give relief "when the grief commeth of a cold," or afford a pleasant hot drink, free of caffeine, at any time of the day. There are many herbs available that are safe and effective; they may be considered a conservative form of treatment, a home remedy that follows the ancient medical precept of "first do no harm." Thus we may enjoy the best of both worlds.

The use of common names for herbs, wild herbs, and garden plants was decided upon in the interest of greater readability. Since this is not a textbook, I feel within my province to choose to do this. Unless one's eyes and mind are trained to recognize plants by their botanical nomenclature, the pleasure in the subject pales for want of understanding. I fully recognize the necessity for proper botanical terminology, indeed wouldn't want to work without it, and therefore it has been included for clarification. The index will list the herbs under their formal and informal names for ready reference. We will meet as friends, on a first-name basis.

With everyone, the pronunciation controversy rages on. Various reputable unabridged dictionaries list "ûrb" first and then "hûrb"; others reverse the order. Interestingly enough, almost every word before and after includes the *h* in the pronunciation. The English pronounce the *h* most definitely; and the Herb Society of America states a preference for the sound of the *h*.

It's really as easy to use the *h* as not. The sound becomes compelling, bearing a certain explicitness I find useful in lectures. But I say, suit yourself. The important point is to renew your acquaintance with these ancient plants, pursue their infinite pleasures, and recognize them for their importance in our lives. To know them is to use them.

So what, exactly, *is* an herb? My favorite definition of the word *herb* is "any plant useful to man that grows in a temperate climate." The important part of this definition is the phrase "useful to man."

I know about the horticultural reference that restricts herbs to herbaceous plants arising from the earth in spring and then withdrawing in the fall. I've also encountered the definition that places seeds, roots, and barks in yet another separate category. Then there's the one that limits their usefulness to fragrance, medicine, or seasonings.

To be so limited! Hippocrates lists 400 plants in his *materia medica,* of which some 200 are still listed officially and in use today. Many of these medicinal plants are fragrant; others are insect repellent, dye plants, seasonings, plants of multiple usage. It would be difficult to sort them out according to one limiting definition or another. The significant difference, that which sets these plants apart and makes them important, is their usefulness. *An herb is a useful plant.*

So, when you hear of an herb garden with over 200 plants, you can see they are abiding by the broadest definition, which I prefer. We shall employ this thinking in this book and include as many of the plants found useful by the early Americans as feasible. We shall be using a simple definition that works.

Seeds, roots, flowers, barks, fruits, and leaves; annual or perennial; trees, mosses, shrubs, and vines are all part of the parade of herbs. When you read through the lists of herbs, you may be surprised to learn that you are already tending a herb garden — peony, iris, hollyhock, yucca, hen and chickens, barberry, roses, and willow — just a few of the herbs important to this story. Cloistered walls protected all these and more, willingly tended for their valuable "benefits."

Never were people more dependent upon plants than when those first self-exiled saints and strangers settled on the shores of this new fierce territory. The interdependency of plants and people now assumed life-and-death proportions to a degree equaled in later years only by the trek west.

Our frontier heritage has had a profound influence on all of us. Leaving the past behind and starting anew seems basic to the American dream, for we are still doing it. The English, Scots, Swedes, French, Germans, and all those others who came to these shores brought their customs along, moved them across the country as the age of exploration and migration progressed. Although they ostensibly left the past behind, the first thing they did in their new world was to re-establish the old ways, old customs, old ideas. As people moved west to start their new life, fraught with unknown dangers and hopeful possibilities, their ties with the past were revealed in their dress, holidays, mores, gardens, and use of herbs. We can relate to the colonists through our own gardens, where the same herbs are nurtured, gathered, and preserved.

Today space-travel concepts make all this look tamely old-fashioned. However, to me, a spacecraft with its well-trained, highly educated team backed by a multimillion-dollar complex of technology in no way pales the frontier achievements, where every man was on his own, responsible for his welfare and that of his family, in a strange and terrible terrain, under unique circumstances, always living with great danger.

Now we are again reviving frontier thinking and living. Disillusioned with inner-city living, the hazards of lawlessness, smog and crowds, traffic and inflation, young adventurers are seeking a new, less complex way of life. Asserting great independence, they are leaving the cities and suburbia, going back to the earth to make it on their own self-reliance, with gardens, farm animals, crafts, and herbs. It is the twentieth-century frontier.

Shunned by many for the greater part of the 1900s, herbs have come out of the past into the present, becoming part of the space age, to take their place side by side with instant everything, miracle drugs, and better living through chemistry. The demand for information on the timeless subject is pleasant assurance that herbs are here to stay.

I enjoy collecting antique recipes and household hints from days long past, but it's not a practical approach to the use of herbs in today's life-style. Therefore in this book we have a sprinkling of old-time recipes, hints, and quotes, but most of them have been updated to incorporate ingredients, standard measures, and equipment available in modern kitchens. The herbs themselves, however, are timeless.

This book is based upon the premise that herbs were vitally important to the founding of this country—the herbs that were found here in this veritable Eden rediscovered as well as those that were brought and made "hereditary in the new land." They are plants of history, herbs rooted in the past and flourishing now in the present, always useful, forever ageless.

Olden days is a relative term. When our small children asked, "What did they do in the olden days when you were a little girl, Mommy?" I had to brace myself to give a civil reply. It's hard to think of three or four decades back as "olden days." But this book covers olden days as I knew them and those extending back to the time of the Indians.

As we stroll through this verbal garden of herbs, back through the paths of time, we will explore native plants and their benefits, folklore and superstition, sometimes whimsical, sometimes based on fact, always fascinating. We will tread a complicated knot garden from witchcraft to spacecraft, discovering the new in the old in infinite variety. It is a garland of herbs, a source of pleasure, with endless suggestions for use, a guide for growing and, hopefully, for inspiration. You will find it a mixture of the old and the new for today's living. And yet who's to say which is the old? This book will, no doubt, seem quaintly antiquated to my grandchildren. They will find here amusing expressions, recipes in need of adaptation, an old-fashioned life-style. Who knows what miracles will come forth in their lifetime, some perhaps to be found in the unprobed mysteries of the unpretentious herbs? It makes us ponder the query, "When did the past end?"

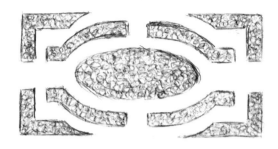

The Herbs
the Colonists
Found Here

NEW ENGLAND RARITIES DISCOVERED
By John Josselyn, Gentleman
printed in London, 1672

Cabbidge growes there exceeding well

Lettice

Parsley, Marygold, French Mallowes, Chervil, Burnet,

Winter Savory, Summer Savory, Time, Sage, Carrots,

Parsnips of a prodigous size,

Red Beetes,

Radishes

Purslain

Pease of all sorts and the best in the world. I never heard
   of nor did see in Eight Years time one worm Eaten Pea.

Spearmint, Rew will hardly grow

Featherfew prospereth exceedingly.

Southernwood is no plant for this Country, Nor Rosemary,
   Nor

Bayes,

White Satten groweth pretty well, so doth
Lavender Cotton. But
Lavender is not for the Climate.
Penny Royal,
Smalledge
Ground Ivy or Ale Hoof.
Gillyflowers will continue Two Years.
Fennel must be taken up and kept in a Warm Cellar all the Winter.
Housleek prospereth notably,
Hollyhocks.
Enula Campana, in two Years time the Roots rot,
Comferie with white Flowers,
Coriander and
Dill and
Annis thrive exceedingly, but Annis Seed as also the Seed of Fennel
    seldom come to maturity; the Seed of Annis is commonly eaten
    by a fly.
Clary never lasts but one Summer, the
Roots rot with the Frost,
Sparagus thrives exceedingly so does
Garden Sorrel and
Sweet Bryer or Eglantine
Bloodwort but sorrily but
Patience and
English Roses very pleasantly.
Celandine by the West Country Men called Kenning Wort grows
    but slowly.
Muschata as well as in England.
Pepperwort flourisheth notably and so doth Tansie
Musk Mellons are better than our English and Cucumbers.
Pompions there be of several kinds; they are dryer than our English
    pompions and better tasted; You may eat them Green.*

The lists of herbs that were here first have been scattered
through hundreds of years of assorted horticultural literature.
Like many family records, unless assembled and written down,
they are lost. Let's bring them back together.

Squawroot, mayflower, mountain tobacco, Dr. Culver's root,
and yellow jessamine; passionflower, buffalo berry, beach plums,
wild grapes, snakeroot, and pipsissewa, a litany of herbs indigenous to this vast land, the foods and medicines of those who lived
here first and those who settled it later—these are the native

---

*This is the list of plants carried from England to American gardens, where some
flourished, some did not, as it was printed originally.

plants of immense benevolence to be set apart and given a separate place in history. For they were here when the settlers arrived.

A home plantation of native herbs was not necessary; the fields, woods, meadows, and streams were the first American herb gardens. To give space in your herb garden to pleurisy root, fringe tree, bayberry, or joe-pye weed is to honor our rich American horticultural heritage and to recognize its significant part in establishing colonies, expanding frontiers, promoting commerce between our land and the rest of the world.

The herb garden dedicated exclusively to native plants would be a naturalized garden, shared by wild flowers, shrubs, and trees grown as they would abide naturally, with wooded areas, filtered sun, paths to stroll into open sunny places, as one finds in nature.

For those involved in restoration projects, the search for plants native to this land is not always an easy one. Escapes from gardens have made themselves at home across the country; whole fields of daisies, Queen Anne's lace, battalions of dandelions, buttercups, lawns filled with plantains, and roadsides heaped high with day lilies, all have become American wild flowers. None of us can remember when this cheerful roll call of familiar flowers

*Photo, by Russ Hamilton, courtesy of Office of
Public Information, Ithaca, New York*

The Robinson York State Herb Garden, at Cornell University, where 800 species, including native herbs, are grown.

were not with us. They too have their place, but not on this native plant list. They are the naturalized citizens of our countryside.

Indian squaws and medicine men used hundreds of herbs, gathered freely. Their knowledge was developed over centuries of life in America and complete familiarity with native herbs. This knowledge then was transmitted to the settlers, perhaps by chance, perhaps by teaching, perhaps by observation. Much of it was subsequently carried back to the Old World, where American herbs quickly became welcome additions to European *materia medica*, new treatments for stubborn ailments grown resistant to old familiar medications. Sassafras, passionflower, gelsemium took Europe by storm, promptly finding their way into monastery gardens, apothecary shops, their herbals.

Particularly interesting to restoration projects, museums, folklorists, and medical historians, the list beginning on page 23 was compiled from many sources over a long period of time simply because a native American herbal as such does not exist. The subject has interested me ever since the day, many years ago, when I learned that the common tawny day lily was an escape from someone's garden, not indigenous to this land. How could that be? One saw them everywhere! They have become "hereditary in the new land." I have been separating natives from newcomers ever since.

Wild-flower gardening is the easiest of all kinds if you respect the likes and dislikes of the plants. "Don't plant a field flower in a wooded area" is an oversimplification. It has always been one of my favorite gardening tenants to use in the landscape those plants that naturally grow well in the area. For instance, the bayberry that achieved such magnificent proportions in our New Jersey garden falters and limps along here in Pennsylvania, producing berries reluctantly, a shadow of the bayberry we formerly knew as a weed. Therefore, to develop a naturalized area with greatest success observe what is growing well around you. To experiment with other plants, give them the soil, moisture, exposure, and climatic requirements necessary, to the best of your ability. Sometimes a little microclimate can be simulated — a pocket of cool moist earth for marsh marigolds or a sunny southern spot where rosemary can be wintered over or cactus coaxed to thrive, bloom, and set fruit.

In recognizing these plants for their original importance to the health and well-being of our settlers, I am not suggesting for one moment that we return to log-cabin medicine or foraging for our food, although I don't denigrate either idea. To my way of thinking, that would be a step backward and living the hard way. The good old days are over; the appellation "good" occurs only in retrospect. "New" is not always better either, but rather to be weighed in the balance, perhaps to be rejected. To select the best of the old, retain the skills, crafts, lore, knowledge of herbs, and spirit of the pioneers — this is our rich heritage. Combined with the new, it's the best of both worlds.

In the listing of our native American herbs, I have deliberately eliminated lengthy descriptions. A good wild-flower guide will suffice in this respect. Detailed descriptions plus sketches or photographs and certainly a knowledgeable guide are essential on any weed walk. In all cases, avoid ingesting plants of uncertain identification, especially those with medicinal properties, unless you really know what you are doing.

Plants as medicines are frequently unpredictable, dependent upon growing conditions, plant variety, time of harvest, part used, method of preparation, and dosage — all variable factors. This warning is given only because plants *are* effective.

NATIVE AMERICAN HERBS

Alder (Alnus crispa) (A. rugosa). A good red dye obtained from the bark. A bitter tea for colds, stomachaches, and diarrhea. Native to swampy areas of eastern United States.

Alder, Black (Ilex verticillata). Also called winterberry because of the clusters of bright-red berries on bare stems in winter; native to eastern United States; valuable because its roots act to help drain wet soils.

Alum Root (Heuchera americana). Also called American sanicle; the raw roots are astringent; a plant of the woods; used to stop diarrhea; cousin to *Heuchera sanguinea*, the coralbells of our gardens; from eastern United States.

Angelica (Angelica atropurpurea). Not the same angelica grown in herb gardens, although similar; slightly poisonous, although used medicinally; boil in several waters to use; can be used in salads; to 9' tall; from Canada to West Virginia; (also *Angelica lucida*).

Arbor Vitae, American *(Thuja occidentalis).* Native to northeastern United States; the oil is insect-repellent; tea of the flat lacy leaves used medicinally by early settlers; attractive ornamental in landscapes.

Arbutus *(Epigaea repens).* Called mayflower or trailing arbutus; the whole plant was used medicinally; diuretic, astringent; requires very acid soil; beautiful wild flower; blooms quietly under oak leaves in May.

Arbutus   *flame Azalea*

Arnica *(Arnica montana).* Called mountain tobacco; perennial; thistle with daisylike flowers; medicinal (used with extreme caution; poisonous in large amounts).

Arrowhead *(Sagittaria latifolia).* Commonly found across North America; edible roots used as potatoes by the Indians in Oregon; a water plant with arrow-shaped leaves.

Ash, Mountain *(Sorbus americana).* Beautiful clusters of bright-orange berries, high in vitamin C; used as an antiscorbutic; Indians used it for treatment of heart diseases; American cousin to "the Rowan Tree," which was considered protective; found in the woods from Labrador south to North Carolina and westward.

Aspen, Quaking *(Populus tremuloides).* The leaves are in constant movement; the bark contains salicylates, as in willow, used for pain; grows from Canada through western United States; inner cambium layer is edible raw or cooked.

Asters, Hardy *(Aster* sp.*)*. Lovely wild flower; blooms in almost all colors except yellow; indigenous to most of the United States; taken to England, where they hybridized it into the Michaelmas daisy.

Azalea, Flame *(Rhododendron calendulaceum)*. A brilliant flowering shrub that blooms in May; from Pennsylvania south to Georgia; now used ornamentally in the landscape.

Azalea, Pink *(Rhododendron nudiflorum)*. The "pinxterbloom," beloved flower of wooded areas; sometimes in gardens.

Balsam Fir *(Abies balsamea)*. Source of turpentine; the bark and twigs as a herbal tea, with honey, for rheumatism; a rub for sore muscles; only species native to northeastern United States.

Bay, California *(Umbellularia californica)*. Named because of its similarity to the true bay; large seedpods gathered and stored to use as nuts, always roasted; leaves used medicinally for headaches and stomach problems; also burned to "fumigate a house"; the leaves are sometimes marketed for *Laurus nobilis,* which they closely resemble, labeled California Bay Laurel.

California Bay   Beebalm

Bayberry *(Myrica cerifera)*. An evergreen native shrub with gray berries that yield a wax used in candle-making; called candleberry and also wax myrtle because it is like the true myrtle, fragrant and evergreen; from Newfoundland to Florida; medicinal, the bark of the root.

Beach Plum *(Prunus maritima).*   Native on coastal areas from Maine to Virginia; fruit purple to black, delicious; found by the Pilgrims on the shores of New England. To make beach plum jelly, add a cup of cold water to each pound of ripened fruit, well washed. Bring to a boil, crush, and cook for 30 min.; strain; then add 1 c. sugar to each cup of juice and boil hard to 220°. Skim and pour into sterilized jelly glasses; cover with paraffin.

Bearberry *(Arctostaphlos uva-ursi).*   Also called manzanita, red bearberry, or kinnikinnick; an evergreen with bright-red edible berries; found in northern American woodlands; frontiersmen used the dried leaves in their tobacco; medicinally a diuretic; used in tanning leather.

Bear's Foot *(Polymnia uvedalia).*   Native to New York through Michigan south to Florida; leaves shaped like a bear's foot; the root used medicinally for malaria; also as an ointment.

Bee Balm *(Monarda didyma).*   Or Oswego tea; used as tea by Oswego Indians, who taught the settlers to drink it; red flowers, a tall mint attractive to hummingbirds and bees; must be boiled to extract full flavor.

Beech, American *(Fagus grandifolia).*   Handsome gray-barked tree of woods of eastern seaboard and as far west as Texas; used to make small woodenware, furniture, and as charcoal; small nuts are sweet and edible; eaten by Indians and early settlers; light-gray bark and horizontal limbs outstanding in any forest, especially in fall.

Beechdrops *(Epiphegus americana).*   A parasite on the beech tree roots; used medicinally, called cancer root.

Birch *(Betula alba* and sp.).   Native to most of the United States; twigs make a tea; bark used medicinally; favorite chewing aid to hunger, much used by Indians; the trees can be tapped like maples, the sap boiled into a syrup; before farm machinery did it, American farmers brushed their harrowed fields with birch trees dragged by horses to prepare fine seedbeds.

Bitter Root *(Lewisia rediviva).*   State flower of Montana; beautiful in flower although small; plant of mountain ranges of the West; named for Lewis of the famous expedition; roots used as food by Indians and early pioneers.

Blackberry *(Rubus villosus; R. allegheniensis).*   Best known of the wild and cultivated blackberries; many species, all delicious, sought out by man and beast; leaves used medicinally, as a tea.

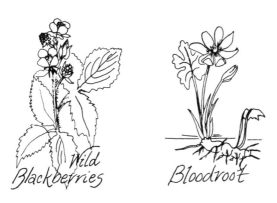

Wild Blackberries   Bloodroot

Black Cohosh *(Cimicifuga racemosa).*   Also called squawroot, snakeroot; used as an insecticide; root used medicinally; Indians used the tea of the root during childbirth; externally as a woundwort.

Black-Eyed Susan *(Rudbeckia hirta).*   Popular wild flower sometimes grown in gardens; golden daisylike flower of summer with black centers, much used in dried arrangements; native to eastern North America.

Black Haw *(Viburnum prunifolium).*   Bluish-black fruits, sometimes eaten; one of the high-bush cranberries; a tea of the berries or bark was used medicinally for ulcers.

Black Indian Hemp *(Apocynum cannabinum).*   Resembles dogbane; grows wild in pastures, fields of Northwest; usually avoided by livestock because of its bitter juice; the Indians used the root medicinally.

Black Root *(Leptandra virginica).*   "Culver's Root"; introduced as a medicinal plant by Dr. Culver, who used the root as a purgative; an Indian remedy.

Bloodroot *(Sanguinaria canadensis).* Fresh root used for pneumonia and other chest disorders; a dye plant; used by the Indians to paint their bodies.

Blue Cohosh *(Caulophyllum thalictroides).* Also called squawroot; grown throughout the United States; near streams; the root used medicinally, a tea for relief during childbirth.

Boneset *(Eupatorium perfoliatum).* Called Indian Sage; grows throughout the United States; bitter tea made from leaves; used cold as a tonic, hot as diaphoretic; used by settlers for colds.

Buckeye *(Aesculus glabra).* Ohio buckeye. *(A. californica).* Western buckeye; the buckeyes, when properly pretreated, were used as food by western Indians; popular shade tree, formerly much used to line streets; the fruit was used to stupefy fish enough so that they could be caught by hand.

Buffalo Berry *(Shepardia argentea).* Grows throughout United States and Canada; eaten by birds; silvery leaves, red berries; gathered and eaten by Indians, raw or cooked, especially with roasted buffalo; also for jellies; sometimes dried.

Bunchberry *(Cornus canadensis).* Low-growing member of dogwood family; white flowers, red berries; woodlands throughout northern United States, New England to Alaska; eaten by birds, animals, early settlers.

Butterfly Weed *(Asclepias tuberosa).* Called pleurisy root; showy native milkweed; grows along sunny roadsides; brilliant orange flowers in June, difficult to transplant because of the tuberous root and because it sets seeds infrequently— an endangered species; root used as indicated by common name, considered a remedy for children's pneumonia.

Butternut *(Juglans cinerea).* Sometimes called white walnut because of its white heartwood, used in furniture; the nuts are eaten; brown dye made from inner bark and husks; midwest United States; tea from the bark; sap harvested for syrup.

Cactus *(Opuntia sp.).* Also called Indian fig; the fruit 2″ to 4″ long, yellow to red to purple when ripe, with a sweet pulpy content, edible; beautiful yellow flowers bloom on old pads; the cochineal insects (valuable plant dye) feed on these.

Calamus *(Acorus calamus).*   Also called sweet flag because of its resemblance to wild iris and its fragrant root; has a small yellowish spadix, a distinctive flower, halfway up the flowering stalk and at right angles to it; highly aromatic rootstocks used as fixative in potpourri; also eaten as a substitute for candied ginger; also as a fragrant moth repellent much used by pioneers.

Camas *(Camassia quamash).*   Pretty blue wild flower native to the wet meadows of the west coast; large bulbs harvested in great quantity, baked 24 hours, then eaten as food (or dried for later use).

Butterfly Weed   Carolina Allspice

Carolina Allspice *(Calycanthus floridus).*   Sometimes called strawberry bush or spicebush or sweet shrub because of the fragrance of the dark-brown flowers; ladies of old carried the flowers tied in handkerchiefs to sniff during church services; the reddish-brown flowers are petals and sepals; native from Virginia south to Florida but hardy farther north; mentioned as early as 1690; called powder bush; when dried, the green leaves crumble into a fine dust, which was used as baby powder during the depression; so common in old gardens and so beloved that it is frequently called just plain "shrub."

Cascara Sagrada *(Rhamnus purshiana).*   A small tree, 20' to 30' high, native to western United States; the bark provides

29

a popular laxative drug which is gathered in the wild by judicious pruning; an important economic botanical because it yields several products from purgatives to tonics.

Catalpa *(Catalpa bignonioides).* Handsome shade tree with lovely white blossoms in June and long cigar-shaped fruits in fall and winter; supposedly Indians smoked them; native to the central states, it grows easily everywhere.

Cattail *(Typha latifolia).* A native bog plant of many uses; edible tubers and young shoots; mats woven from the leaves; the down was used in pillows and quilts; also leaves were used as caulking between barrel staves; throughout the United States and Canada.

Century Plant *(Agave* sp.). Also called mescal; native to southwestern United States; flower buds gathered as food; ripe seeds ground made a flour; also a fiber plant, especially for bowstrings.

Century Plant

Chia

Chapparel *(Larrea divaricata).* Called creosotebush, greasewood; a bitter herb used medicinally; 1 T. leaves equals one 15 gr. tablet; also used in artificial vanilla.

Cherries, Wild *(Prunus virginiana).* Called chokecherry; native to almost entire country and Canada; fruit for wine, jellies, food for birds and game; young thin bark used as a cough medicine, especially popular in cough drops.

The Herbs the Colonists Found Here

Cherry Laurel *(Prunus caroliniana)*. Native evergreen with shiny black fruits; from Virginia south; handsome ornamental in the landscape.

Chestnut *(Castanea dentata)*. Tall tree to 100'; several nuts of good flavor in a prickly burr; leaves and inner bark used medicinally.

Chia *(Salvia columbariae)*. Native to the Southwest; annual sage; valuable to Indians, Mexicans, and the pioneers, who harvested the prolific seeds for a thirst-quenching drink and a highly nutritious food; the seeds sprout readily and can be used like cress in salads; the seeds are high in vegetable protein, a source of endless energy.

Clematis, Wild *(Clematis virginiana)*. Virginsbower; native east of the Rockies; grows and blooms profusely in silvery clusters that become white seed puffs; ornamental.

Columbine, Wild *(Aquilegia canadensis)*. One of our loveliest wild flowers; grows profusely on rocky outcroppings; red and yellow color harmony; a tea made from the seeds was an old Indian remedy for headache.

Coralberry *(Symphoricarpos orbiculatus)*. Native from New Jersey south and west to Texas; dull coral-red berries in winter; now planted extensively along highway banks; the powdered root was once used as a remedy for malaria.

Coralroot *(Corallorrhiza odontorhiza)*. Native from Maine to Florida; a leafless plant with fleshy tuberous roots; parasitic on the roots of trees; entire plant used medicinally.

Coreopsis *(Coreopsis lanceolata)*. Eastern United States; other varieties from southern and western United States; a cheerful native golden daisy, sometimes double; useful in gardens.

Corn, Indian *(Zea mays)*. Common Indian corn, indigenous to North and Central and South Americas; a food staple, of enormous economic importance; each kernel has a small husk, then the whole ear is enclosed in a husk; colorful; the silk used medicinally as a tea.

Cranberry *(Vaccinium macrocarpum)*.   Many varieties, all edible berries; a woody evergreen with red fruits; grows in bogs; harvested with comblike scoop after frost; native to northern tier of states south to North Carolina; used in pies, jellies, sauces similar to domesticated varieties.

Cranberry, Highbush *(Viburnum trilobum)*.   Tall shrub with flat dull white flowers followed by brilliant red berries that look like cranberries; throughout northern states; delicious fruit, gathered before frost while plump and firm.

Cranesbill *(Geranium maculatum)*.   Wild alum; the dried root is sold commercially for its astringent properties.

Currants *(Ribes sanguineum)*.   Northwestern North America; *(R. odoratum)*. Buffalo currant, central United States; edible berries used by wildlife, Indians, and early settlers; jams, jellies, wine, cakes, and dried for winter.

Damiana *(Turnera aphrodisiaca)*.   Texas and lower California and South; a small shrub with highly aromatic odor; the leaves used medicinally as a stimulant.

Dewberry, Eastern *(Rubus flagellaris)*.   From Canada to the Gulf of Mexico; shiny black fruit, edible.

Dewberry, Southern *(Rubus trivialis)*.   From Virginia south to Texas; used as parent plant for other varieties.

Dewberry, Western *(Rubus ursinus)*.   Native to Pacific area; usually black, sometimes white or red; used as raspberries.

Dock *(Rumex hymenoseplus).* Large perennial weeds; grow everywhere; called wild spinach or wild pie plant and used in the same ways; Indians, Eskimos, and pioneers sought out these wild greens.

Dogbane *(Apocynum androsaemifolium).* Indigenous to the United States and Canada; a milkweed with large bitter root; juice said to remove warts.

Elderberry *(Sambucus canadensis).* A shrub widely grown from the Rockies east; many kinds; flavorful fruit used by early settlers because of similarity to European elders; still gathered for pie, wine, jelly, leaves as tea.

Elm *(Ulmus fulva).* Red elm or slippery elm; upper New York south to Florida; inner bark has a mucilaginous quality; used in salves, poultices, and as a tea or gargle for sore throat; pioneers ate the bark in a kind of gruel for nourishment; also made a support from elm for the Liberty Bell in Independence Hall, Philadelphia.

Foamflower *(Tiarella cordifolia).* Favorite wild flower; indigenous to the woodlands of the east coast; ground cover.

Franklinia *(Gordonia altamaha).* Discovered in the wild by John Bartram along the banks of the Altamaha River in Georgia; never found in the wild since 1790; a horticultural mystery.

Fringe Tree *(Chionanthus virginicus).* Loose clusters of white fringed flowers bloom in May; colonists used the bark of the root as a laxative and as a tonic; now grown as an ornamental; native from Virginia south to the Gulf of Mexico.

Fritillary *(Fritillaria sp.).* Native to eastern United States; yellow fritillary and other kinds have edible starchy roots.

Galax *(Galax aphylla).* A stunning evergreen ground cover in the mountains of Virginia through Georgia; the decorative leaves gathered and used by florists.

Garlic, Wild *(Allium canadense).* Common throughout Canada to Florida, west to Texas; all wild onions are edible, all parts, depending upon your taste; used by the Indians and the pioneers to flavor foods; makes a zesty wild vinegar.

Gentian, Fringed *(Gentiana crinita).* Beautiful biennial native to eastern North America; blooms in fall; bright blue; don't pick or dig! Rare; endangered.

Ginger, Wild *(Asarum canadense).* Found across the northern half of the United States and Canada; handsome aromatic ground cover in well-drained woodlands; unusual brown cuplike flowers; roots used by colonists as a substitute for ginger, dried and ground; or whole and candied as a sweet; also in tea.

Ginseng, American *(Panax quinquefolium).* A fleshy rooted herbaceous perennial indigenous to hardwood forests from Maine west to Minnesota and south to Georgia; sometimes grown under cultivation; much prized, especially in Oriental countries, for the medicinal value of the root; ginseng opened up our trade with the Orient during the colonial period; mentioned in Jefferson's records for its medicinal use.

Goldenrod *(Solidago sp.).* Used for stomach disorders and the kidneys, especially *Solidago odora,* the fragrant goldenrod, commonly known in Pennsylvania as Blue Mountain Tea; the Hopi and Navaho dye plant; Indians used the powdered leaves for wounds, externally; has a gall which, when cut open in winter, yields a grub used as bait; common North American wild flower of late summer and fall.

Golden Seal *(Hydrastis canadensis).* Formerly abundant, this native perennial grows in open woodlands from Ontario south to Kentucky; the rootstock is much sought as a medicinal plant and has been harvested extensively; the leaves are also gathered; Cherokees used it to treat arrow wounds.

Golden Seal   Hawthorn

Grapes, Wild *(Vitis* sp.). America has many kinds of wild grapes, found all through the United States; gathered for jelly, wine, desserts, juice, et cetera; abundant; sometimes called fox grapes, scuppernong; vigorous vines produce a favorite food for animals, birds, and man; pick after frost for best flavor.

Groundcherry *(Physalis pubescens).* Common wild plant, with bright-yellow fruit enclosed in a papery lantern-shaped husk, first green, then beige; eaten raw or cooked, especially pickled; all through the United States.

Groundnut *(Apios tuberosa).* Plant found from east coast to Colorado and south to New Mexico; edible large tubers kept the Pilgrims alive during that first dreadful winter; also called wild bean because the vine produces edible beanlike seedpods; propagated by seeds or tubers.

Hackberry *(Celtis occidentalis).* Sweetish berries were dried and ground by Dakota Indians and used as a seasoning for meat; an interesting twiggy shrub subject to "witch's broom"-type growths; pithy hollow stems; eastern United States.

Hawthorn *(Crataegus* sp.)*.* Small thorny tree with white double flowers in spring and attractive red berries in fall; native from Virginia south to Alabama; planted at Monticello as a fence; the berries are edible, jams and jellies especially welcomed by early settlers; Washington's Thorn is *Crataegus phaenopyrum.*

Hazelnut, American *(Corylus americana).* Wild through east and central United States; *C. cornuta* indigenous to southern states; shrubs or trees; nuts used as food; also in baking; planted in fence rows where cows can nibble on the leaves to increase butterfat; also aids their digestion; cows rest under the trees, where they are less bothered by flies.

Hellebore, Green *(Veratrum viridis).* Also called false hellebore or American hellebore; native to low grounds; perennial; the rhizome used medicinally, but a powerful poison.

Hemlock *(Tsuga canadensis).* Eastern hemlock; bark used as a dye; produced turpentine; Indians pounded bark into a poultice; tea from new growth; state tree of Pennsylvania; NOT poison hemlock.

Hepatica *(Hepatica americana).* Indigenous to North America and Canada; whole plant considered tonic; used for lung ailments; much loved wild flower of spring.

Hickory *(Carya* sp.)*.* North American trees with edible, highly desirable nuts; Indians made a liquor from the powdered nuts and shells; tall tree; wood used for implements.

Holly, American *(Ilex opaca).* Pyramidal evergreen with dull green leaves and bright-red berries; much used decoratively at Christmas; the Indians roasted the leaves and used them as a tea; crumbled dried leaves used as a coffee substitute; believed to remedy colds.

Holly, Myrtle-Leaved *(Ilex myrtifolia).* Small-leaved native holly; shrub with bright-red clustered berries; native through the Carolinas to Florida.

Holly, Swamp *(Ilex decidua).* Native from Virginia south to Florida and west to Texas; deciduous; most interesting when the berries are visible in winter; also called winterberry and possumhaw.

Honeysuckle, Coral *(Lonicera sempervirens).* Brightly colored trumpet-shaped flowers; ornamental vine; blooms May through August, Massachusetts south to Florida and west to Texas.

Hop, American *(Humulus americanus).* Native to central and western United States; similar to European hop and used in the same ways; has been introduced into Oregon hop yards and grown commercially; for tea, yeast, beer.

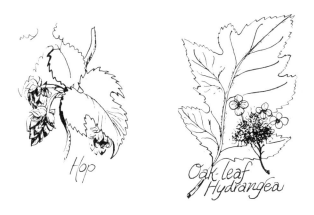

Hop-Hornbeam *(Ostrya virginiana).* Sometimes called iron-wood because of sinewy trunk; a smooth wood; inner wood used for fever and ague; native to eastern United States.

Huckleberry *(Vaccinium pensylvanicum).* A low evergreen shrub with blue-black fruits, much desired; used by Indians and settlers; also called whortleberry and billberry; common throughout the entire United States. *V. corymbosum* is the high bush blueberry; eaten for jellies, muffins, pies, and as fruit.

Hydrangea *(Hydrangea arborescens).* Tree hydrangea; native to eastern United States below New England; white flowers; magnificent vine when planted as an ornamental. *(Hydrangea quercifolia).* Oak-leaf hydrangea; the dried root, fresh leaves, and young shoots are used for kidney and bladder ailments.

Indian Physic Root *(Gillenia stipulata).* All through North America east of Alleghenies; the bark of the root is used; purgative; Indian remedy.

Indian Pink *(Spigelia marilandica).* Also called pinkroot; native perennial found from New Jersey south and west to Texas; grows in wooded shade and moist soil; root gathered by the Cherokees, sold commercially, used medicinally.

Indian Pipes *(Monotropa uniflora).* Found in moist wooded areas across the continent; a root parasite springing up at the base of trees; unique because of its absence of chlorophyll and ghostly appearance; Indians used the entire plant as a sedative in cases of extreme hysteria.

Indian Tobacco *(Lobelia inflata).* Grows in the Great Lakes region; blue flowers; dried leaves used medicinally by the Indians; a potent drug plant, poisonous.

Indian Tobacco

Jack-in-the-pulpit

Indigo, Wild *(Baptisia tinctoria).* Southern and eastern United States; bluish-black pods used in dried arrangements; the bark of the root and leaves were used by desert tribes of Indians as an all-around medicine; the plant is dried to yield a blue dye—a poor substitute for indigo.

Inkberry *(Ilex glabra).* A native deciduous holly; small shrub; black berries used as an ink substitute.

Ironweed *(Vernonia altissima* and sp.). Found in the East through the Midwest; purple flowers in late summer; the root and leaves were used for diseases of the skin.

Jack-in-the-Pulpit *(Arisaema triphyllum).* Found in eastern North America from Canada to Florida and west to Minnesota; favorite wild flower; the dried roots are powdered into an edible flour; the seeds are eaten by wild fowl.

Jerusalem Artichoke *(Helianthus tuberosus).* Not an artichoke and certainly not from Jerusalem; native from Nova Scotia to Georgia; grown for its tuberous roots, boiled and eaten as potatoes, also raw; one of the few vegetables cultivated by the Indians, who taught the earliest colonists to use these as substitute potatoes; also called Canada potato, girasol; to 12′ high.

Jerusalem Oak *(Chenopodium ambrosioides).* From the American tropics, now common throughout the United States, in vacant fields, along railroad tracks; attractive chartreuse foliage, dries well; seeds and herb used to expel worms; effective in the treatment of poison ivy, as an infusion.

Jessamine *(Gelsemium sempervirens).* Carolina jessamine; William Bartram remarked that this prospered on top of cold hills in South Carolina and yet froze in winter in Pennsylvania; fragrant yellow tubular flowers in early spring; evergreen; a sweet-smelling ornamental; used medicinally, a homeopathic remedy for reducing fever, more effective than aspirin.

Jewelberry, Purple *(Callicarpa americana).* Beautiful clusters of purple berries which attract birds; Indians used it for malaria and dysentery.

Joe-Pye Weed *(Eupatorium purpureum).* Distributed through northeast and middle United States and Canada; tall perennial with pale lavender flowers in fall; root used medicinally for many ailments; called Queen of the Meadow.

Juniper *(Juniperus virginiana).* Eastern red cedar; also other cedars; such as western red cedar *(J. scopulorum).* The seeds are used to flavor gin; a dye plant; sometimes used medicinally as a stimulant or a diuretic; from Alaska south to Mexico; berries eaten by wild game birds. Boil the berries — a few only — to make a palatable tea. Considered a remedy for gout, sciatica, dropsy, and to hasten childbirth; useful to veterinarians; also as a seasoning, mostly for wild meats.

Kentucky Coffee Tree *(Gymnocladus dioicus).* Large native tree; very fat hard pods which hold seeds that Kentucky pioneers used as a substitute for coffee; grown now as an ornamental.

Knotweeds *(Polygonum bistorta* and sp.*).* Common weed throughout the country; animals browse on it; Indians and early settlers lived on the young shoots, the leaves and stems, tuberous roots.

Labrador Tea *(Ledum groenlandicum).* Also Hudson Bay Tea; an evergreen shrub with fragrant leathery leaves used as a tea, especially during American Revolutionary period; native from upper Canada south through Great Lakes region and Pennsylvania.

Lady's Slipper *(Cypripedium pubescens).* North American woodlands; flowers late spring; the roots were employed by the Indians for nervous afflictions and hysteria.

Larch *(Larix americana).* Beautiful deciduous evergreen; common to eastern United States and Canada; inner bark makes a tea, stimulant, laxative, and useful as an eyewash.

Linden, American *(Tilia americana).* Also basswood; Canada south to Alabama and Texas; heart-shaped leaves, fragrant white flowers attractive to bees; Indians used the fibrous bark to make rope; flowers and leaves make a pleasant tea, good for colds, fevers, or as a poultice on swellings.

Live Oak *(Quercus virginiana).* Native from Virginia south to Mexico; very broad, horizontal boughs; extremely hard wood used for wooden ship construction; the Indians thickened their venison soup with the ground acorns.

Lizard's Tail *(Saururus cernuus).* Whitish flower spikes curl at the end, suggesting its name; plant of the swamps of eastern United States; adapts to life in the garden as a perennial of some interest.

Lobelia, Great Blue *(Lobelia siphilitica).* Tall perennial; can be transferred to the autumn garden; deep-blue flowers; eastern United States.

Lobelia, Scarlet *(Lobelia cardinalis).* Cardinal flower; scarlet-flowered tall perennial; blooms in moist shaded places in late summer; eastern United States; a choice wild flower.

Locust, Black *(Robinia pseudo-acacia).* Native from Pennsylvania through Georgia; tall trees with lacy compound leaves; trunks used much as poles and fencing, which has been known to sprout; a tree legume; locusts help build up the soil of dying forests.

Locust, Honey *(Gleditsia triacanthos).* Large tree to 130'; compound leaves and large thorns; long twisted pods once used as food; the interior sugary pulp of the seedpod was made into a sweet drink; native from Pennsylvania west to Nebraska and south to Texas.

Honey Locust   Southern Magnolia

Madrone *(Arbutus menziesi).* Called also Oregon laurel; beautiful tree native from British Columbia to lower California; Indians taught the settlers to eat the berries, use the bark and leaves for soothing ointments, as a tea for colds. Taken back to Spain during the early exploratory period, it is the official tree of Madrid.

Magnolia, Southern *(Magnolia grandiflora).* Large glossy evergreen leaves, much prized as decorations; white cup-sized flowers set this magnificent tree apart; grown as an ornamental from Virginia south, where it is native.

Magnolia, Swamp *(Magnolia virginiana).* Also called sweet bay; native from Massachusetts through Texas; sometimes evergreen; the leaves resemble the true bay; very fragrant white flowers in spring; roots and bark were used as a tonic; also as a substitute for quinine; sometimes called swamp magnolia or swamp laurel.

Maidenhair Fern *(Adiantum pedatum).* Native to deep woods of northeastern United States and Canada; herb used for colds and coughs; a lovely curved fern easily naturalized in wooded gardens.

Maple *(Acer* sp.). Sugar (several species produce sugar); swamp; red; the sweet juice harvested by tapping in early spring and boiling out the water; a major industry in colonial days; revived interest because of wartime rationing and, presently, inflationary high prices of sugar; seeds edible; in olden days apples, carrots, and potatoes, all such root crops, were stored separately between layers of maple leaves to help in their preservation; 30 to 40 gallons of sap boils down to 1 gallon of syrup; native from Canada to Florida and to the Midwest.

Mariposa Lily *(Calochortus nuttalli).* Also called sego lily; native high in the Sierra Nevadas; the bulbs were harvested in great numbers by the Indians; Mormon settlers used them as food.

Marsh Marigold *(Caltha palustris).* Common to eastern United States; *(C. leptosepala).* New Mexico to Alaska; spring wild flowers of the lowlands of the North American continent; leaves edible in spring after parboiling in several waters.

42

Mariposa Lily   *Marsh-Marigold*

Mayapple *(Podaphyllum peltatum).*   American mandrake; eastern North America; roots brewed into a purgative, used in very small doses; also the same can be used as a spray for potato bugs; the little apples make charming pomanders; ground cover in large wooded areas from Canada to Texas.

Mesquite *(Prosopis juliflora).*   Small trees or shrub; used by Indians as food, housing poles, firewood, a dye plant, and a medicine; native from Colorado through Texas and lower California.

Milkweeds *(Asclepias* sp.).   The milky juice was an Indian cure for warts. *Asclepias tuberosa* is called pleurisy root; native to the United States and Canada; perennial; young sprouts are edible; also young pods, after bitter milky sap is boiled off; the Indians also used the root for rheumatism.

Miner's Lettuce *(Montia perfoliata).*   Western wild flower which the Indians taught the gold rush '49ers to eat in order to subsist and to help prevent scurvy; a purslane.

Missouri Primrose *(Oenothera missouriensis).*   Day blooming; annual; dazzling sulphurous yellow flowers; central United States, a favorite garden flower in the prairie states.

Monarda *(Monarda fistulosa).*   Pale-lavender wild flowers; members of the mint family; attractive to bees; a strong tea; the Choctaws made an ointment which they used for chest colds; Maine to Louisiana.

Mountain Laurel *(Kalmia latifolia).*   American mountain laurel, considered a prize to send abroad to England and France; the Indians made crude spoons from the wood. At camp we sought out the knobby roots of dead bushes to sand and polish, transformed them into letter openers. State flower of Pennsylvania; native to the northeastern United States.

Mountain Mint *(Pycnanthemum incanum).* Eastern United States; about 18 varieties; hardy, perennial; members of mint family; dense flower heads, whitish; small fragrant leaves; tea plant.

Mulberry, Red *(Morus rubra).* Small tree; fruit used in pies, jellies; also for birds; native from the Northeast to Texas.

New Jersey Tea *(Ceanothus americanus).* Also called Indian tea, walpole tea, and redroot; from Canada to South Carolina; shrubby with white flowers, not over 3' high; shipped to Europe during colonial days and intensely hybridized; leaves used as tea during American Revolution.

Oak *(Quercus* sp.). Indians gathered hundreds of pounds of acorns per family each year; acorns were grated, powdered, eaten by the Pilgrims during the first hard winters; roasted and ground as a coffee substitute; the oil used as a liniment; powdered nuts also used for diarrhea; wood used for furniture, shipbuilding; found throughout the United States.

Missouri Primrose

Oak

The Herbs the Colonists Found Here

Oak, Canyon *(Quercus chrysolepis)*. Indians ground acorns and used the flour in bread; also for soup; bark used in tanning; as a dye plant; western native.

Oak, Willow *(Quercus phellos)*. Native to eastern seaboard from Long Island south; small narrow-leaved tree, attractive in landscaping.

Oregon Grape *(Mahonia aquifolium)*. Northwestern United States; berries make a jelly; roots produce a yellow or brown dye; used as an ornamental.

Osage Orange *(Maclura pomifera)*. From Missouri through Oklahoma; used by the Indians as bow wood; also the thorny thickets were planted as enclosure hedges for cattle during colonial days. Make great pomanders, a substitute for rare oranges; source of orange and green dye.

Papaw *(Asimina triloba)*. Grows wild from New York state through the Midwest to Texas; a small tree that likes shade; the fruit is edible; look like stubby little bananas; smell like strong bananas; called custard apple in the central states.

Papaw   passion flower

Partridge Berry *(Mitchella repens)*. Low-growing evergreen with small leaves, little white double flowers which form one bright-red berry; found abundantly from Canada to Texas; berries are edible; terrarium plant; the entire herb was taken in boiling water as a tonic; astringent.

45

Passionflower *(Passiflora incarnata)*.   Native from Virginia to Texas; called maypops; Spanish so impressed by floral configuration, related all parts to Christ's passion through symbolism; sedative tea from leaves, flowers; a vining plant with edible yellow fruits.

Pecan *(Carya illinoensis)*.   Native throughout Mississippi Valley south to Iowa; nuts used in baking; have been bred extensively for quality of nutmeats and thinness of shell.

Pennyroyal, American *(Hedeoma pulegioides)*.   Paul Wieand, in *Folk Medicine Plants used in Pennsylvania Dutch Country*, calls this "the mosquito plant" and also says, "Years ago it was the king of medicinal herbs." A minty tea, good for digestion and mildly stimulating; bunches of pennyroyal were brought indoors to repel mosquitoes.

Peppergrass *(Descurainia pinnata)*.   A common California weed; the seeds gathered for use as food; a tea was used medicinally by the Indians.

Persimmon *(Diospyros virginiana)*.   Native to eastern United States; a tree with a distinctive bark because of large sections overlapping like shingles; produces a colorful orange fruit highly edible only when completely ripe; self-pruning; the colonists made a potent beer from yaupon and persimmon.

Persimmon   Pokeberry

Phlox *(Phlox paniculata)*, southern United States, summer phlox. *(P. pilosa)*, eastern United States, prairie phlox. *(P. subulata)*, New York to North Carolina, ground pink. *(P. divaricata)*, eastern United States, blue phlox. Many other varieties. Now highly hybridized and used as garden perennials.

Pickerel-Weed *(Pontederia cordata).* Water plant indigenous to eastern United States; blue spikes in June; heart-shaped leaves.

Pine, Virginia *(Pinus virginiana).* Two short heavy needles to a bundle; native from New York to Alabama; used for woodwork.

Pine, White *(Pinus strobus).* From Newfoundland to Georgia; native to the Blue Ridge region; five blue-green needles to a cluster; Indians used the inner bark, ate it raw or cooked; the colonists gathered and dried the inner bark, pounded it into a flour; also the young needles made a tea; important timber tree.

Pinyon *(Pinus monophylla).* A one-leaved pine native to the west coast; an important food, cones gathered by Indians for the valuable seeds eaten dried or roasted; the resin was used on cuts, wounds, or boiled as a tea for colds; low-growing conifer; frequently ancient.

Pipsissewa *(Chimaphila umbellata).* Small evergreen that grows in wooded areas; named by the Indians who used the whole plant for stomach, kidney, and bladder troubles; also called prince's pine; native throughout nearly all of North America.

Plum, Wild *(Prunus americana),* eastern native, small fruits. *(P. augustifolia),* Chickasaw plum, a bush. *(P. a. Watsoni),* sand plum, grows in arid areas. *(P. hortulana),* midwestern small tree, red fruit. All above are edible; used in jellies, wine.

Poison Ivy *(Rhus radicans).* No real reason to include this among plants useful to man except it is a native plant that is listed by the Tradescants as having been collected and shipped to England and also because it is its own antidote; the Indian method of immunity was to chew one of the first new leaves very early in spring.

Pokeberry *(Phytolacca americana).* Native to eastern United States; a handsome wild plant; shoots gathered in early spring as a vegetable; the root and purple berries were used medicinally; also as an ink during the Civil War (called inkberry); taken back to England and introduced as a vegetable.

Pond Lily *(Nymphaea odorata).*   Showy summer flower of still waters throughout the United States; Indians ate the roots roasted or boiled; also dried as meal.

Poplar *(Populus* sp.).   From Canada through entire United States; animals eat the seed and bark; contains salicylate used to reduce fevers; inner bark can be powdered into a flour.

Poppy, California *(Escholtzia).*   Golden yellow annual; state flower of California; now naturalized in eastern gardens.

Prairie Turnip *(Psoralea esculenta).*   Indian breadroot; western United States throughout the Rockies; root edible raw or roasted; used by early explorers to maintain life.

Pumpkin *(Curcurbita pepo* and var.).   Large fruits used as food; were dried and pounded into a meal; origin unknown; tropical species but part of the Indian culture found here by earliest settlers.

pumpkin   *Redbud*

Ragwort, Golden *(Senecio aureus).*   A common weed; native to eastern United States; also called liferoot and swamp squawweed; used medicinally; groundsel.

Raspberry *(Rubus idaeus).*   Many varieties grow throughout the United States; like moist shade; fruit gathered for jams, jellies, wine; all edible; leaves make a pleasant tea, especially useful for women; sometimes called black raspberry or blackcap; also American red raspberry.

Red Bay *(Persea pubescens)*. Native evergreen from Virginia south; resembles the true bay; wood used in furniture; ornamental.

Red Buckeye *(Aesculus pavia)*. Tree with handsome red flowers and dark-brown horse chestnuts; the bark and root have a soaplike extract used as a soap substitute in early times.

Redbud *(Cercis canadensis)*. Native over a wide range from Canada to Texas; heart-shaped leaves; magenta pealike blooms appear with dogwood; buds and blossoms are edible.

Red Chokeberry *(Aronia arbutifolia)*. A spring flowering shrub; native to eastern United States; white flowers; red berries, edible.

Redwood *(Sequoia sempervirens)*. Extremely high, to 340'; native to northern California and southern Oregon; magnificent forests; valuable timber tree.

Rhododendron *(Rhododendron carolinianum)*. Handsome evergreen; native to North Carolina; ornamental. *(R. maximum)*. Large evergreen to 25'; eastern North America; called Rose Bay.

Rice, Wild *(Zizania aquatica)*. Eastern North America; tall grass to 10'; a natural delicacy growing in shallow waters; seeds harvested by beating the bushes; called Indian rice; birds eat the seeds; served as rice.

Rock Rose *(Helianthemum canadense)*. Indigenous to the United States; likes dry sandy soils; yellow flowers in May; whole plant was used medicinally, a bitter astringent.

Rose Acacia *(Robinia hispida)*. A tree legume; locustlike leaves; hairy red stems; multiple leaves and lovely pink locust-type flowers; eastern United States; ornamental that does well in poor soil.

Rose Mallow *(Hibiscus palustris)*. Also called swamp mallow, sometimes marshmallow; a marsh plant of the eastern seaboard; large leaves and hibiscuslike flowers in white through shades of rose.

Rose, Prairie *(Rosa setigera).* State flower of North Dakota; single-flowering pink rose; one of many native roses used for fragrance and edibility; varieties called Baltimore Belle and Queen of the Prairies.

Prairie Rose

Sassafras

Rose, Swamp *(Rosa palustris).* Single-flowered wild rose; pink; grows throughout eastern United States; blooms in June; edible flowers and rose hips (seedpods).

Rose, White Cherokee *(Rosa laevigata).* State flower of Georgia; vigorous growing rose with edible flowers and hips; hips (or haws) make jellies, jams, tea; roots used as stock for hybrid roses for southern climates.

Sarsaparilla *(Aralia nudicaulis).* Wild or Virginia sarsaparilla; used by Indians; the root used as a cough remedy; to flavor drinks, soda (other similar-tasting plants are used as substitutes, i.e., smilax, moonseed); the tea is very thirst-quenching. (True sarsaparilla is indigenous to Central America, Mexico, and the West Indies.)

Sassafras *(Sassafras officinale).* Native from Canada through Texas; called tea tree; twigs used as toothbrushes by settlers; bark of the root used as spring tonic tea; a dye plant; bark also insect repellent; twigs and leaves used, with thyme, to make gumbo file, a seasoning and thickening agent for famous Louisiana soup.

Saxifrage *(Saxifrage punctata* and sp.). Common little plant prone to growing on rocks; from Pennsylvania through Appalachians; leaves are edible.

Scurvy Grass *(Cochlearia officinalis).* Northern Canada, Alaska, and Arctic shores; high vitamin C content; eaten raw or cooked; sometimes grown in gardens as a salad green.

Senna *(Cassia marilandica).* Native to eastern United States; wild or American senna; stout perennial; Indians used it medicinally, as a cathartic, for poultices, and to reduce fevers; the drug "senna" is made from the dried leaves.

Sequoia, Giant *(Sequoia gigantea).* Huge trees native to western United States; some over 2,500 years old; largest conifer in the world.

Shadbush *(Amelanchier canadensis).* Eastern North America; small tree or shrub with many threadlike petals early in spring, at the time the shad run up the rivers to spawn; also called Juneberry, shadblow, serviceberry, sarviceberry (they are being sold under this last name as a tree for city streets); berries were eaten by Indians and early settlers.

Silver-Bell Tree *(Halesia carolina).* Tree to 20'; native from West Virginia to Florida and west to Texas; perfectly hardy in south-central Pennsylvania, where it grows in my garden; blooms April-May with thousands of little bells, in pairs, along every twig.

Skullcap *(Scutellaria lateriflora).* Found throughout eastern North America, Connecticut south to Florida; perennial, pale-blue flowers; the whole plant is helpful for nervous afflictions.

Skunk Cabbage *(Symplocarpus foetidus).* Earliest sign of spring; common in low areas of northeastern United States; large dried root was used for epilepsy and convulsions; handsome woodland plant with strong odor of skunk.

Snakeroot *(Aristolochia serpentaria).* Virginia snakeroot; Pennsylvania south to Texas; many-branched root system; gingery fragrance; root used in treatment of snakebites, also as a stimulant.

Solomon's Seal *(Polygonatum commutatum).*   Native to northeastern United States and Canada; long arching 1½′ stems, with oval leaves, small white flowers; later blue-black berries; the root used to whiten the skin and remove freckles.

Sour Gum *(Nyssa sylvatica).*   Eastern United States; oval waxy leaves turn brilliant orange-red in fall; clusters of small sour berries; tupelo is the Indian name; a bee tree, valuable to honey crop.

Sourwood *(Oxydendrum arboreum).*   Called sorrel tree; attractive small tree with lily-of-the-valley-like flowers followed by hard fruit capsules and bright fall coloration; ornamental; native in eastern United States.

Spicebush *(Lindera benzoin).*   Common from Maine through Michigan to Kansas; highly aromatic leaves; small bush-tree; once used as a tea; if you do this, simmer the leaves, twigs, bark, and berries.

Spiderwort *(Tradescantia virginiana).*   Day flower; introduced to England in 1617, ten years after founding of Jamestown; a most important plant today because the chromosomes are readily split and resplit, and are valuable to the study of heredity.

Spikenard *(Aralia racemosa).*   Perennial; native from Canada south to Georgia; roots used to flavor root beer; purple berries made into jelly; Indians used the root as food; also as cough medicine.

Squash *(Curcurbita maxima).* Again, origin unknown but found here with the Indians; many varieties; excellent food; abundant.

Star Grass *(Aletris farinosa).* Low-growing attractive native; the root was prepared with squaw vine to prevent miscarriage.

Stewartia *(Stewartia malacodendron).* Small tree or shrub; native to southern United States; white cuplike flowers in late spring; ornamental.

Stillingia *(Stillingia sylvatica).* Southern United States; silvery leaves, yellow flowers; perennial; long taproot used as an alterative.

Stoke's Aster *(Stokesia laevis).* Pretty native; southern United States; grown now in northern perennial borders; fluffy lavender heads of many petals.

Spiderwort   Stoke's Aster

Stoneroot *(Collinsonia canadensis).* From Canada to the Carolinas; in moist woodlands; named for Peter Collinson, British botanist; strongly lemon-scented, it is not citronella, although sometimes called by that name; used as a tonic.

Strawberry *(Fragaria americana).* Throughout the United States, except in deserts; William Bartram found this "in painted beds of many acres surface" in Georgia; he called it "Fragrant strawberry"; as desserts, fresh or cooked; a tea from the leaves; settlers as early as 1623 named the shores of New Hampshire "strawberry banks" because of the wild strawberries growing there.

Sumac *(Rhus canadensis)*. Planted as an ornamental; fragrant; not poisonous. *(R. glabra)*. Staghorn sumac; beautiful clusters of fuzzy red berries; velvety gray bark; useful in dried arrangements in winter; the berries make a delicious tea similar to pink lemonade (Indian); also as a Navaho dye plant; colonists gathered and dried the berries; tonic and diuretic; eastern North America. *(R. toxicodendron)*. The poisonous variety.

Sun-Dew *(Drosera rotundifolia)*. Carnivorous plant; common to the bogs of North America; glisten with dew on sunny days; the entire herb is used for tobacco cough; as a stimulant.

Sunflower *(Helianthus annuus)*. State flower of Kansas; raised for its seeds; Indian dye plant, also food; found in sunny open areas through the United States, especially the Midwest; food for game; used also for the oil; also as medicine; roasted seeds a healthy snack.

Sweet Fern *(Comptonia asplenifolia)*. Small shrub with fragrant leaves; throughout eastern North America; a tea during the American Revolutionary period; grows in fields, sometimes edges of woods; likes dry places; actually not a fern.

Sweetgum *(Liquidamber styraciflua)*. A native of wide range; the resinous sap is fragrant only in southern climates where it is collected and used as incense; wood used for furniture; star-shaped leaves; spiny ball fruits.

Wild Strawberry

Sweet Gum

Sweet Pepperbush *(Clethra alnifolia)*. Maine to Florida; summer-blooming shrub with spikes of small off-white flowers;

fragrant; attractive to bees; lovely in the landscape of gardens.

Sycamore (Platanus occidentalis). American plane tree or buttonwood; common native along streams; planted on city streets; distinguished by its peeling bark and broad grayed leaves; shade tree; Jefferson wrote, "My house is embosomed in high plane trees"; and so, praise be, is ours!

Tobacco (Nicotiana tabacum). Annual; native to South America; long, broad leaves for smoking, chewing, snuff; the gold the early settlers were promised in the New World turned out to be tobacco; a quick cash crop much in demand abroad; also used medicinally; as an insect repellent in gardens.

Trillium (Trillium pendulum; T. erectum; T. grandiflorum). Called beth root, wake-robin; roots used as a dye plant; also in cancer research; used medicinally by the Shakers; sold as "Southern John the Conquerer," a charm; an Indian love charm; associated with the Trinity because of its triplex parts; Canada to North Carolina and Missouri.

Trumpet Vine (Bignonia radicans). Orange-red trumpets bloom in early summer; most attractive to hummingbirds; compound leaves; creeps and climbs with aerial rootlets; strong vine; Pennsylvania to Florida, Missouri to Texas; found covering chicken houses and other farm outbuildings; decorative.

Tulip Tree (Liriodendron tulipifera). Also tulip poplar; eastern United States; popular as an ornamental because of shade and unusual green-orange flowers in spring; bark used in treatment of fevers such as malaria; also used to make Indian canoes.

Turkey Corn (Corydalis firmosa). Also squirrel corn; native from Canada to Kentucky; charming small plant; root resembles a corn kernel; medicinal; blue-green leaves and purplish flowers early in spring.

Turtlehead (Chelone glabra). Pink-lavender flowers; grown in colonial gardens; an Indian herb, used as a vermifuge.

Violet (Viola sp.). Native from Canada to Carolina; prolific small perennial of woods and fields; much loved for its ap-

Turkey Corn   Violet

pealing flowers in shades of violet; leaves and flowers used medicinally as a tea.

Virginia Creeper *(Parthenocissus quinquefolia).* Also called American ivy; rampant-growing five-leafed vine; spectacular in fall; used medicinally; tea of the leaves said to assuage drunkenness; New England to Mexico.

Wahoo *(Euonymus atropurpureus).* Burning bush or spindle tree; beautiful in fall, with red leaves; interesting barked twigs; root used medicinally as a bitter tonic.

Wild Yam *(Dioscorea villosa).* Native Rhode Island to Florida; vining plant with fleshy underground roots; heart-shaped leaves; drooping clusters of white flowers; mostly decorative; the dried root used medicinally (the yams grown for food need a long growing season and hot weather, as in the South).

Willow, Black *(Salix nigra).* Used medicinally by pioneers, instead of aspirin, for pain and fevers; all varieties; throughout the United States; charcoal from the willow made the finest gunpowder.

Wintercress *(Barbarea vulgaris).* Hardy from Alaska throughout the North American continent; easily grown, early green; valuable antiscorbutic; can be eaten fresh or boiled as a vegetable; grows all winter.

Wintergreen *(Gaultheria procumbens).* Used for flavoring; twigs, leaves, berries as tea; for colds and as a tonic; chew on the berries too; eastern United States, upper Great Lakes to Georgia; pretty woodland plant; aromatic.

Wistaria, American *(Wistaria frutescens).* Small-flowered version of the more commonly cultivated Chinese wisteria; native from Virginia south; named after Dr. Caspar Wistar, an eighteenth-century Philadelphia physician.

Witch Hazel *(Hamamelis virginiana).* Archaic, Wych-Hazel; shrubby small tree, reminiscent of the hazel of Europe; gathered forked twigs to use for diving water; twiggy growth, golden "twisted ribbons" of flowers in November when other trees are bare; sun or shade; difficult to grow from seeds; mild astringent; cooling to bites, swellings; antiseptic; lotion made from the twigs; the twitching dowsing forks gave it its common name, presumed to "be possessed"; not related to hazelnuts.

Yaupon *(Ilex vomitoria).* Native evergreen holly with long blunt leaves; red berries in fall; Indians made a "black drink," very strong and emitic; used as a beer when combined with persimmons, herbs, and fermented; contains caffeine; Virginia to Florida, west to Texas.

Yellow Lotus *(Nelumbo luteum).* A fine stand of this disappearing native is protected at Tabernacle Creek, Virginia Beach (Lotus Festival held there in July); native from Florida to mid-Atlantic states; flowers and leaves rise 4' above water; decorative seedpods.

Yellow Wood *(Cladrastis lutea).* Native to the mountains of Tennessee, Kentucky, and North Carolina; has pealike white flowers in spring; a dye plant, yellow from the wood.

Yerba Buena *(Satureja douglasi).* Also Oregon tea, a species of savory with a mintlike flavor; the herb for which San Francisco was first named; native to the Pacific Coast, the "good herb" was much used by Spanish settlers medicinally and as a tea.

Yerba Santa *(Eriodictyon californicum).* The Indians taught the Spanish settlers how to use this native western weed; as a tea for colds and lung complaints; as a poultice for man or beast; leaves were chewed along their travels as a thirst quencher.

Yucca *(Yucca filamentosa).*   Native in southeastern United States, North Carolina to Florida. *(Y. aloifolia).* Spanish bayonet; southern United States to Mexico; now grows everywhere; handsome perennial with stiff rosette of leaves and stately inflorescence; leaves used as hemp, in weaving baskets, combined with furs or linen to make fabrics; juice used to degrease new wool; also as a shampoo; fruit as food.

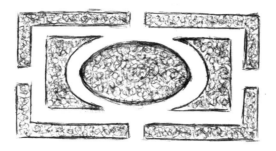

Early American Gardens

"There is no softer trait to be found in the character of these stern men than that they should have been sensible of these flower roots clinging among the fibers of their rugged hearts, and felt the necessity of bringing them over seas, and making them hereditary in the new land." — Nathaniel Hawthorne in *The American Notebooks*

COLUMBUS TO THE COLONISTS

A colorful map of early America painted by a Spanish conquistador shows early plantations and settlements surrounded by forests in which colonists are gathering quinine and tending prickly pear cactus, a plant cultivated for food and for the red dye produced from the cochineal insects living on the spiny pads. An old Indian pictograph shows aloes being grown and eaten. Bits and pieces such as these help bind together the story of early American gardens.

Convinced the world was round and that the Spice Islands could be reached by crossing the Atlantic, Christopher Columbus led his small Spanish fleet of three in search of a short route to the Orient. After a seemingly endless voyage, they landed on what he called San Salvador. Thinking his quest for gold and spices to be successful, the explorer thought it to be an outpost of "the Indies" and called the natives "Indians." Only after his third successful crossing in 1498 was the discovery conceded to be an "Other or New World," later called America.

After all the native heirlooms had been seized and the search for gold abandoned, they turned to other things for profit, including plants. Columbus brought back to Europe tobacco, corn, medicinal plants, and some spices. There is a record that sassafras bark was carried in the pockets of inhabitants of Seville to repel insects. Our native passionflower, mysteriously beautiful and sedative, assumed a prime position in the monastery gardens of Europe and promptly found a place in the writing of early herbalists.

On his second voyage Columbus brought seventeen ships with 1,200 colonists, horses, sheep, goats, pigs, cattle, orange and lemon trees, wheat and barley, seeds, and grapevines. His Spanish patrons, also evangelists committed to conversion, pressed all Indians over the age of fourteen into service and taxed each one several pounds of cotton or a small amount of gold. If the Indians were unable to pay, they were made to serve as forced laborers to the settlement.

In 1513 Ponce de Leon landed near this site of what was later Saint Augustine, the oldest colony in America, where walled patios and concealed gardens are still favored, as they are in California and the Southwest—reminders of those first settlers and their Spanish culture.

After the defeat of the Spanish Armada, the Atlantic lost its terror and became open seas for the Dutch, for the French, and, even more, for the English; it became a well-traveled highway to Canada and the new English colonies.

Every ship that succeeded in making the perilous voyage returned with cargo, including plant treasures for the gardens of Europe. The French scoured the Canadian wilderness, shipping native plants to the great French arboretums; this explains why many of our indigenous plants are named "canadensis." Many

English botanists visited or settled here to explore and collect the flora of the New World.

Within two weeks of the arrival of English colonists at James-town in 1607, wheat was sown and kitchen gardens laid out. The precious cache of seeds and roots, herbs, vegetables, and grains, so carefully transported, were now snugly transferred to their new home.

Women of the *Mayflower,* in 1620, brought similar packets of seeds with them, mostly herbs and vegetables. They sent back to England for more seeds, especially for woad, a blue vegetable-dye plant, and for familiar medicinal herbs. They tended their kitchen gardens with fierce devotion, carried water, raked the soil, returned animal fertilizers to its natural source, sowed seeds, and harvested herbs essential to their families' welfare.

Early in the 1600s Captain John Smith, who called the northern colonies "New England," landed on an island off the coast of Maine in May and planted a "garden of sallets"—herbs and green vegetables to be harvested and used by the crew of the sailing ship on their way back to Virginia.

The Pilgrims, the Puritans, and the colonists who followed by the hundreds planted kitchen gardens as soon as arrival and weather permitted. The settlers found that America's earliest farmers, the Indians, gardened crudely. Indian gardens were primitive affairs—temporary patches, with corn and pumpkins planted, weeded, and tended by squaws and children, who used stone hacks and digging sticks. In the main the Indians were con-tent to harvest foods growing in the wilderness—acorns, wild nuts, berries, and greens.

By 1676 shipbuilding became a thriving industry in America, thanks to the abundance of hard-oak forests. At that time there were 730 ships in Boston alone; the industry soon grew to 2,000 vessels sailing the oceans, whaling, transporting goods up and down the coast, and, in an endless procession of ships, traveling well-charted routes back and forth to England and the Con-tinent. They brought people, plants, and supplies; the ships re-turned with "timber, tobacco, pitch, potash, sturgeon, and caviare."

Gardening in colonial America reflected the background of the gardener; each nationality pursued land husbandry as it had been practiced at home. The colonists planted the same mint and thyme and angelica in Boston and Williamsburg as that which had grown in their gardens in England.

According to early records, the Swedes set out fruit orchards in lower New Jersey in 1665; the Dutch who settled New York in the early 1600s brought garden vegetables; the English brought fruits such as quinces, orchard cherries, peaches, apricots, plums, almonds, and apples; the Germans planted good grapes for wine.

The Scotch-Irish and the Germans, in their quest for religious freedom, followed William Penn to Pennsylvania, where fertile soil, timber, and game provided them a home. The Pennsylvania German hausfrau planted, then as now, small patches where every inch was made productive — a proper kitchen garden. If one pushed aside the sage plant, he'd find potatoes growing. Dill was sowed next to the radishes, and by the time the radishes were pulled, the dill would be ready to take over the area. Pole beans climbed sweet-corn stalks; pumpkins sprawled between; here and there there was a clump of mint for tea or a stray calendula for first aid. Savory, the bean herb, called "bohnengreidle," would grow there too, along with the beans it graced.

Thousands of ships now traveled the ocean, bringing settlers with their livestock for meat and milk along with the grain to feed the animals. Small and crowded, the ships took from six to twelve weeks to make the trip. There was little to eat and drink along the way; death was their constant companion. Journeys frequently took even longer, depending upon winds and weather and beset by the dangers of pirates and the sea. When the horrors of the voyage ended, the self-exiles faced famine, sickness, and much hard work.

This country had been advertised in superlatives — the trees, flowering vines, strawberries, fruits, corn, melons, an abundance of berries, food for the gathering — a paradise. It hardly prepared the colonists for the actuality with which they were greeted: the curious, not always friendly natives; the bitterly cold weather in the north; the hardships and sickness that reduced their numbers to half and less.

When winter and weather, illness and savages came crashing in on them with terrible inexorability — a life we can barely imagine — it was the garden to which the settlers turned. Every home built — or, when necessary, rebuilt — embraced the land essential to the task of gardening. Building the shelter and planting the garden—these were the first things to be attended to.

As changes came slowly in the colonies, the villages enlarged into towns and the houses grew apace. The families increased and prospered; the Indians were less terrifying. And so the gardens grew larger, more formal, more colorful, more enjoyable. Now surrounding fields, outside stockaded areas, were also apportioned and cultivated.

Since money was scarce, coins were almost nonexistent; so the barter system was employed. The herbalist had a ready market for her surplus harvest; it was a valuable commodity to be traded for other goods and services necessary to her household. The Yankee Peddler came into existence, traveling old Indian paths now turned into roads, his cart loaded with wares for those who settled beyond the town areas. He also carried herbs from the north to the south and back again. He had indigo for dyeing, medicinal jessamine and passionflower from the south; he exchanged it in the north for tansy, sassafras, bloodroot, and Shaker medicines, selling it as he trod his course.

As more and more settlers arrived in ever-increasing numbers, the settlements pushed farther west into Ohio and beyond. Pioneers heading west took with them packets of seeds and grains, precious treasures, herbs necessary to life, for food, for "the kindly healing herb," for flavor or dyeing, for fragrance, and, hopefully, for pleasure.

All the hope of the nation was contained in those packets of seeds, transported across the ocean or across the land at such peril, planted with depths of emotion hard to recapture in today's luxurious way of life.

The history of this country and the herbs found or brought here are interwoven into a colorful tapestry of linen and wool and cotton, all dyed with plants and created by thousands of industrious hands. Beginning with the search for the rich spices of "the Indies" that led to the discovery of America, from that time on no ship left these shores without a bounty of plants useful to man. The herbs of America proved as rich a treasure as the spices of the original search.

In turn, the herbs brought here were those transported to England by the Romans or to Spain by the Moors; indeed, they were the very ancient herbs of the Bible, the herbs extolled by early herbalists, the same herbs beloved by Shakespeare and the poets. As world trade flourished, the commerce in plants increased and the gardens of early America, both wild and cultivated, were central to this trade.

THE SUPERABUNDANCE OF THIS COUNTRY

Colonists, Pilgrims and Puritans, settlers and frontiersmen, scouts and guides, missionaries, plant explorers, homesteaders, forty-niners, and all the pioneers who explored, expanded, and settled the vastness of America were dependent upon the wilderness and its bounty while, paradoxically, engaged in conquering it.

Our fields and woods, prairies and deserts, mountains and rivers yielded enormous quantities of foods and herbs for their many needs. Of the estimated 8,000 plants found growing here in America, only half a dozen or so were then known in England and Europe. Early botanists and plant explorers were kept busy discovering, collecting, and shipping back everything they found growing wild in this new lush paradise. The wilderness was a treasure of incalculable horticultural wealth to be exchanged for the goods available from the Old World. Collecting native seeds and plants occupied all our first botanists. John Bartram of Philadelphia, Mark Catesby and John Custis of Williamsburg, John Clayton, and many other "Procurers of Plants and Encouragers of Gardening" relayed a steady stream of plants, seeds, bulbs, and roots to and from England and the continent to Europe. No ship arrived without people and the plants necessary to their welfare; no ship returned without a greater exchange of plants indigenous to this country.

Traveling plants became the concern of the ship's captain, certain ships being favored over others for this task. The small sailing ships took six to twelve weeks of travel, the plants requiring space, water, and care during all that time. Along the way rain water was collected for this purpose. John Evelyn set down the following guidelines for gathering and shipping plants:

"The seedes are best preserv'd in papers: their names written on them and put in a box. The Nutts in Barills of dry sand: each kind wrapd in papers written on.

"The trees in Barills their rootes wraped about mosse: The

64

smaller the plants and trees are, the better; or they will do well packed up in matts; but the Barill is best, & a small vessell will containe enough of all kinds labells of paper tyed to euery sort with ye name."

In ordering seeds from England in 1749, William Logan of Germantown cautioned, "Take care the mise don't Eat them . . . don't lett the Salt water wash them."

It's easy to understand the jubilation that greeted a new shipment of healthy plants at either end of the lengthy voyage, and the consternation when a precious root succumbed to harsh weather or seeds failed to germinate properly.

The plant correspondence of Washington, Jefferson, and Penn, as well as that of all the early botanists, is one of our most

Photo courtesy of Plimoth Plantation

An overall view of part of Plimoth Plantation, Plymouth, Massachusetts. Sheep are being herded out of the kitchen garden.

valuable historical legacies. The horticulture of this tumultuous new land generated all manner of enthusiasm for the plants — ways to grow them, export and trade them, catalog them, use them. Exuberant interest in botany abounded.

Hollander lawyer Adrian Van der Donck, for whom Yonkers was named, wrote in his 1653 journal of the settling of New Amsterdam "the superabundance of this country is not equalled by any other in the world." He described such herbs as angelica, violet, iris, coriander, mallow, marjoram, calamus, malva, indigo, and leeks as growing in his own garden.

There was plenty to be found here. The industrious harvesting of native plants by the early colonists was their own reward. Food and medicine were free for the gathering, along with fish, turkeys, and wild game to go with the herbs, fruits, nuts, berries, leaves, and roots. Throughout New England, friendly Indians showed the settlers the way to survival by living off the land, how to plant corn with a fish in each hill to fertilize it, which plants were medicinal.

Wild greens abounded, much sought after, as were all the fresh foods of early spring. Sassafras roots, dug as soon as the ground thawed sufficiently, made a pleasing cup of tea, that first spring tonic after a long hard winter of salted dried foods. American sassafras quickly became the rage of London, where steaming cupfuls were hawked on the streets. Pumpkins, squash, and ground nuts were here, eaten fresh while in season, dried for the rest of the year. Our native tobacco became a main commercial crop for use by the colonists and to be traded abroad, where it was considered a medicine.

In New England the colonists found strawberries, raspberries, cranberries, wild ginger, grapes, blueberries, and codfish. In New Jersey, Pennsylvania, and Ohio they found beechnuts, papaws, many nut trees, and wild cherries. Tobacco, mulberries, holly, yaupon, and persimmons were found in the Middle Atlantic states. The South added pecans, "maypops," and tropical fruits to their diet. The Great Lakes region yielded nutritious wild rice. In the Midwest prairies they found chestnuts, clover, sunflowers. Farther west they welcomed the yucca, barrel cactus, and opuntia fruit, Indian corn and beans. The Rockies were blessed with juniper berries, winter cresses, wild nuts, and plums. Along the Pacific they found squaw tea, desert sage, piñon nuts, and chia.

Everywhere this land produces handsomely—thousands of plants for the use of those brave enough to settle it.

Flowering native plants soon found their way into the settlers' gardens and on board ships for transportation back to the Old World. Wisteria, bee balm, black-eyed Susans, wild blue phlox; passion vine, jessamine, and woodbine from the South; cattails, virgin's bower (wild clematis), columbine, flame azalea, sumac, coreopsis, rose acacia, silver bell tree, trumpet vine, autumn asters, honeysuckle, violets, jewelweed, and turtleweed—a parade of colorful "natives" to cheer the heart, to grace a garden as, indeed, they still do.

ACCORDING TO THE RECORDS . . .

1493: "Pepper [here] more pungent than that from Caucasus." — Peter Martys, member of Columbus' expeditions.

1597: "They [the people of Seville] know not what other to do having cut or hurt themselves but to run to the tobacco as a most ready remedy. It doth marvellous work without any need of surgery but only this herb."—From *Joyfull News Out of the new Founde Worlde,* by Nicholas Monardes, 1597.

1620: "And there came a smell off the Shore like the Smell of a Garden."—John Winthrop, Puritan leader, in his *Journal.*

1630: "1 Iron pot, 1 Kettel, 1 Frying pan, 1 Gridiron, 2 Skellets, . . . 1 Spit."—Rev. Francis Higginson in his advice to new settlers planning to come to America.

1634: "Whereas many died at the beginning of the plantations, it was not because the Country was unhealthful, but because their bodies were corrupted with sea-diet . . ." From *New Englands Prospect,* by William Wood.

1637: "The country there naturally affordeth very good pot herbs and sallet herbs . . ."—From *New English Cannan,* by Thomas Morton.

1670: "The ground is overgrown with underwood in many places and so perplext and interwoven with vines, that who travels here, must sometimes cut through his way."—John Lederer, German explorer, writing near Fredericksburg, Va.

1672: "Birds, Beasts, Fishes, Serpents and Plants of that Country, together with The Physical and Chyrurgical Remedies wherewith the Natives constantly use to Cure their Distempers, Wounds and Sores." — Frontispiece for *New Englands Rarities Discovered,* by John Josselyn.

1682: "Let my children be husbandmen and housewives." — William Penn in a letter to his wife, Gulielma, in England.

1685: "Dr. Henry Woodward is credited with having first procured and dispersed for planting Gold Seed Rice from Madasgascar about 1685. By 1690 the production of rice in South Carolina had so advanced that the planters asked that it might be specified as one of the commodities in which they might pay their quit-rents. By 1700 its production was declared by the Collector of Customs to have been so great that there had not been enough ships in Charles Town that year in which to export it all." — From *A Charleston Sketchbook,* by Charles Fraser.

1690: "[Six acres] for a Playground for the Children of the town to Play on, and for a Garden to plant with Physical Plants, for Lads and Lasses to know Simples, and to learn to make Oils and Ointments." — From the will of George Fox, founder of the Quakers.

1710: "Our daughter began to take drops of ginseng." — From diary of William Byrd of Westover, entry dated December 23, 1710.

1719: "Fresh garden seeds of all sorts lately imported from London . . . as also English Sparrow Grass Roots, Carnation Layer, Dutch Gooseberry and Current-Bushes." — From *The Boston Gazette,* advertisement dated February 28, 1719.

1720: "Planted in Potts, 1720; An Almond Stone, an English Wallnut, Cittron Seeds, Pistachica nutts, Red Damsons, Leamon Seeds, Oring seeds and Daits." — From diary of a Massachusetts bride.

1750: Speaking of the extensive gardens of Mepkin of Charleston: "Enriched with everything useful and ornamental that Carolina produced or his extensive mercantile connexion enabled him to procure from remote parts of the world. Among the variety of other curious productions he introduced olives, capers, limes, ginger, guinea grass, the Alpine strawberry, bearing nine months of the year, red raspberries; blue grapes; and also directly from the South of France, apples, pears, and plums of fine kinds, and vines which bore abundantly of the choicest white eating grape called Chasselats blancs."—From *History of South Carolina,* by David Ramsay, 1809.

1758: "Apple pie is used throughout the whole year, and when fresh Apples are no longer to be had, dried ones are used. It is the evening meal of children."—Dr. Acrelius, a parson, writing home to Sweden.

1760: "The care of plants such as needed peculiar care or skill to rear them, was the female province. Every one in town or country had a garden. Into this garden no foot of man intruded after it was dug in the Spring."—Mrs. Anne Grant, writing of the Dutch in Albany.

1765: "Christmas is come, hang on the pot,
Let spits turn round and ovens be hot;
Beef, pork and poultry now provide
To feast thy neighbours at this tide.
Then wash all down with good wine and beer,
And so with mirth conclude the year."
　　　—From *Virginia Almanack,* Williamsburg, 1765.

1766: "I am making you a charming collection of bulbous roots which shall be sent over as soon as the prospect of freezing on your coast is over. The first of April, I believe, will be time enough for you to put them in your sweet little flower garden, which you so fondly cultivate."—Robert Stockton, writing from England to his wife in Princeton, N.J.

1771: "Yielding and paying therefor unto the said Henry William Stiegel, his heirs or assigns, at the said town of Manheim, in the Month of June Yearly, forever hereafter, the rent of One Red Rose . . ."—Baron William Stiegel, indenture for the gift of land for a church.

1771: ". . . let us abstain from the Use of foreign tea. There is no one article imported so fatal to the Cause of Liberty as this; . . . Were the Ladies of New England truly sensible how much their health is endangered, and consequently their CHARMS by a constant use of this destructive plant, I am persuaded they would need no other motive to induce them speedily to reject it."—From *An Astronomical Diary, Or, Almanack,* by Nathaniel Low, Boston, 1771.

1773: "Observe these green meadows how they are decorated; they seem enamelled with the beds of flowers."—From *Travels of William Bartram.*

1774: "Carolina Magnolia flower trees, the most beautiful trees that grow in America and 50 large Catalpa flower trees; they are nine feet high to the upper part of the top and thick as one's leg."—*New York Mercury* advertisement.

1798: "With regard to our manufacture of cloth women and children commonly dictate the colors to be impressed on them. But they frequently make injudicious choice, the color which they dictate fades, the coat is spoiled and thrown aside."—From *The Country Dyer,* by Asa Ellis, Brookfield, Mass.

1800: "Between 1800 and 1811 Salem enjoyed a virtual monopoly of the Sumatra pepper trade, because of its aggressive shippers, swift vessels, and capable mariners. Salem, then the sixth largest city in the United States, for several years paid an average of five per cent of the nation's total import duties, of whichpeper formed an important part."—From *The Book of Spices,* by Frederic Rosengarten, Jr.

1801: "A Mrs. Loomis, in Connecticut, informed me, that an Indian cured a cancer, by the internal and external use of the juice of white-ash, that issued out of the ends of the wood, as it was burning."—From *American Herbal,* by Samuel Stearns.

1818: "Many troubled with the asthma cut the [colt's foot] leaves small and mix it with tobacco for smoaking, and affirm they found great benefit thereby."—From *Nature the Best Physician; or A Complete Domestic Herbal,* by Joseph Taylor.

1819: "A Right Good Plaster: Take wormwood, Rue, yarrow, and beeswax of each an equal part, but of the beeswax a little more, add tallow and a little spirits-of-turpentine, simmer together in an oven and strain them." — From *The Long Hidden Friend* or *True and Christian Information for Every Man*, by John George Hohman, publisher, Reading, Pa., 1819.

1819: "Balm, or lemon balm alone, or with sage, is much recommended, with a few flowers of lavender; it has a most delicious flavor and taste, but is most agreeable when green" (a tea). — From *Family Receipt Book.*

"Rose leaves dried in the shade, cloves beat to a powder, and mace scraped; mix them together and put the composition in little bags" (to perfume linens). — From *Family Receipt Book.*

1833: "Sage is very useful both as a medicine, for the headache — when made into tea — and for all kinds of stuffing, when dried and rubbed into powder." — From *The American Frugal Housewife.*

1839: "Tarragon should be gathered on a dry day, just before the plant flowers. Pick the green leaves from the stalks, and dry them a little before the fire. Then put them in a wide mouthed stone jar, and cover them with the best vinegar, filling up the jar. Let it steep fourteen days, and then strain it through a flannel bag." — From an old recipe book.

1854: ". . . that elderly dame . . . in whose odorous herb garden I love to stroll some times, gathering simples and listening to her fables . . ." and also: "I am no more lonely than a single mullein or dandelion in a pasture, or a bean leaf, or sorrel, or a bumble-bee . . ." — From *Walden,* by Henry David Thoreau.

1859: "Herb Powder for flavouring when Fresh Herbs are not obtainable: 1 oz. of dried lemon-thyme, 1 oz. of dried winter savory, 1 oz. dried sweet marjoram and basil, 2 oz. of dried parsley, 1 oz. of dried lemon-peel. . . . Pick the leaves from the stalks, pound them, and sift them through a hair-siever; mix in the above proportions, and keep in glass bottles, carefully excluding the air."—From *The Book of Household Management*, by Mrs. Isabella Beeton.

1864: "Cloves, in coarse powder, one ounce; Cassia, one ounce; Lavender flowers, one ounce; lemon peel, one ounce. Mix and put them into little bags, and place them where the cloths are kept, or wrap the cloths around them. They will keep off insects."—From *Godey's Lady Book,* May issue.

1878: "A lump of alum put in the vinegar, and horseradish cut in strips, will make them [pickles] crisp."—From *Mrs. Winslow's Domestic Receipt Book.*

1880: "To Make A Bouquet of Sweet Herbs: Put two sprigs of parsley on the table, and across them lay two bay leaves, two sprigs of thyme, two of summer savory, and two leaves of sage. Tie all the other herbs (which are dry) with the parsley. The bouquet is for soups, stews, game and meat jellies. When it can be obtained, use tarragon also."—From *Miss Parloa's New Cook Book.*

THE SHAKERS: AMERICA'S PROFESSIONAL HERBALISTS

Religious freedom in America is well exemplified by the small communal sect known as the Shakers. A group pledged to celibacy and, inevitably, extinction, they strongly believed that "beauty rests on utility; the highest use possesses the greatest beauty." A small community of Shakers remain, even today.

Simplicity and serenity have always been their way of life. It is reflected in their exquisitely designed furniture, a highly refined utilitarian colonial pattern, so completely functional as to be their greatest legacy to this twentieth century. The Shakers will be memorialized best by the classic form and function of their household furnishings, devoid of ornament, now museum pieces, where the clean designs are much admired and copied.

Although they pursued many ways to make a living—cabinetry, for one—agriculture has been their basic economy. They have lived almost monastically, close to the earth, tending livestock, orchards, vegetable gardens, and fields of herbs and grains. Eventually, in the pursuit of perfection, they eliminated almost all nonagricultural labors as being "too worldly."

They became professional herbalists, the first in this country to put the growing and marketing of medicinal herbs and drug plants on a profitable basis. Their valuable crops were converted into herbal products, ointments, salves, pills, powders, tonics, elixirs, and patent medicines sold throughout the colonies as well as for export — a business that reached its pinnacle by 1820.

The poppy *(Papaver somniferum)* was cultivated assiduously for its invaluable drug crop, opium, the most powerful painkiller known to man. The immature poppy seedpods were first slit and then later revisited to harvest the gummy substance which the Shakers refined into medicinal preparations of opium, morphine, laudanum, codeine, and paregoric. The medicines marketed by the Shakers were beneficial to the wounded on our nineteenth-century battlefields.

Some botanicals they grew to prepare for sale included lemon balm, sweet marjoram, sassafras, pleurisy root (butterfly weed), peppermint, tansy, roses, basil, horehound, sage, thyme, borage, savory, rue, hyssop, pennyroyal, wormwood, and many others, both cultivated and collected, to an approximate total of two hundred.

Starting with the sale of a few surplus seeds from their farms, the good quality of their product soon caught on. They printed their own labels, sewed their own seed bags, made boxes for them, then took the seeds out on loaded wagons and sold them directly to the farmers. By 1790 they conducted the first major garden-seed industry in America.

They also cultivated a special broomcorn in their fields, which enabled them to mass-produce the first flat brooms. The demand for Shaker brooms was so great that by the 1800s it was the start of another Shaker industry.

Everyone in the Shaker communities was expected to work to the degree of his capabilities — tending the gardens, sorting and packaging seeds, drying sweet corn and apples, preparing medicinal herbs for sale. Shaker ladies worked in the herb shops, using herb cutters, stills, sieves, mortar and pestles of their own functional design to process the medicinal herbs they grew.

Their herbal preparations were famous. I have an advertising booklet dated 1889 extolling the merits of Shaker Extract of Roots at 60¢ a bottle, Shaker Soothing Plasters for 25¢ each, and Shaker Family Pills for 25¢. Blessed by good health, the Shakers labored industriously, persevered to live virtuously, without benefit of sinful "superfluities," and prospered thereby for over a century.

SHAKER RECIPE FOR MAKING YEAST

One-half pound of dry hops; pare one dozen of potatoes boil in five quarts of water three-quarters of an hour, drain the juice through a sieve to four and a half quarts of rye flour, stir until the flour is all moist, but not to a paste; set aside to cool; add one teacupful of old yeast, one half teacup of salt, the same of ginger, one-half pint of molasses, mix thoroughly together; be ready to use in twelve hours.

—Recipe from an old advertising brochure,
Shaker Community of Mt. Lebanon, N.Y., 1889.

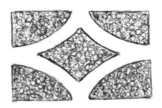

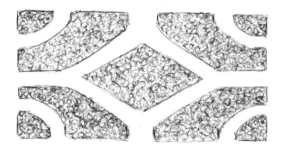

Colonial Herb Gardens

EIGHTEENTH-CENTURY GARDENS

In a land that was extraordinarily wild, the newcomers wanted to imitate their homelands as much as possible, and so they planted gardens. Such gardens were not a luxury but an absolute necessity, giving variety to the diet, providing domestic pharmacopoeia—frequently the only kind of medicine available to the wilderness family. Lives depended upon the herbs they grew in their gardens and the knowledge thereof.

The first settlers' gardens were close to the house, surrounded by hedges or protective fences, kitchen gardens of herbs, potherbs, and vegetables; also, perhaps a few flowers, some old roses and hollyhocks "for use and for delight."

Gardens in Salem, Massachusetts, were neatly laid out in squares or rectangles, reminiscent of England, with "parsley, sweet chervil, sorrel and other pot herbs on one side of the path, and on the other sage, spearmint, mullein, fennel and medicinal

A Heritage of Herbs

herbs." This general arrangement begun in 1620 continued in use during the eighteenth century and is still good today.

Virginia became England extended, a copy of home in architecture and gardens, with all the best-loved shrubs, trees, flowers, and herbs willingly transplanted to the new royal colony. The climate and citizenry were well suited to the cultivation of the earth and its incomparable rewards.

Each colonist was allotted a piece of land large enough for a home and an adjacent kitchen garden. The town, then, was enclosed within a stockade for protection. Fields outside the fenced area produced fruit trees, grain, and larger crops for the entire community. Eventually, as the population of the colony increased and the Indians retreated, settlers moved to larger acreage; house, kitchen garden, and adjacent fields became a one-family farm. The garden close to the home was still the province of the housewife, the fields being tended by the men and farmhands.

By the opening of the eighteenth century, gardens were becoming more formal, quite geometric—an effort to create a con-

Photo courtesy of the Early American Society

This beautiful garden, in Middletown, Pennsylvania, has boxwood around its central bed, which contains a sundial, in the manner of the eighteenth century.

trolled environment in this strange, untamed land that was to be home. Gardens assumed a simple elegance and quiet beauty; they became an artistic expression of the home owner. Greenery was considered restful, a desirable setting for a home. Lawns were developing.

Sometimes, as on large estates, the garden areas were rigidly formal, laid out in prescribed patterns of limited kinds of plant materials — a direct attempt to subdue nature through absolute control of the immediate surroundings. Knot gardens were developed, with closely planted, well-clipped plants of thyme, box, or germander interlaced in intricate patterns. Parterres, a repeated geometric design, an elaboration of the knot garden, were much admired. Personnel necessary to keep boxwood hedges, espaliers, and topiaries well trained and trimmed was available. Such features gave each garden individuality.

Colonial Williamsburg has many eighteenth-century gardens to visit, including several herb gardens to enjoy and perhaps to emulate in part. The Governor's Palace is the most extensive planting, with many pleasure gardens, including a well-clipped labyrinthian maze in which to lose oneself. Terraced down to the canal, it has herbs on the first three levels and vegetables on the remaining, all superlatively maintained.

The John Blair house kitchen garden is laid out geometrically, two diamonds in rectangles, defined and divided by brick walks. It features raised beds with rosemary that seems constantly in bloom, edgings of thyme, groupings of other herbs and pansies in spring. The George Wythe garden is a gem, showing all that can be accomplished with half an acre in the heart of a town. George Wythe believed that herbs were to be used, so he grew them next to his garden area in utilitarian rows. His barn was filled with herbs, hanging and drying. This is a garden of peace and purpose, a place to work and, when there's time to rest, to look up through the greenery at the spire of Bruton Parish Church rising in the distance.

At Mt. Vernon, George Washington had two large garden areas balancing his estate plan — one a pleasure garden, the other a kitchen garden. Jefferson's Monticello includes another splendid garden typical of the large planting of wealthy landowners. These homes and gardens are open to the public today, prime examples of the great abundance of edibles and ornamentals available to the gardener in this country during the eighteenth century.

William Penn, leader of the Quakers, founder of Pennsylvania, built his home above Philadelphia on the Delaware River in a quiet place where the world does not yet intrude. There, with his gardeners from England and Scotland, he developed extensive gardens, using many native trees and shrubs dug from the wilderness, as well as fruit trees, seeds, roots, and, according to his diary, eighteen roses ordered from England. The reconstructed garden at Pennsbury Manor is large, with a generous variety of herbs to the left of the brick walks and vegetables to the right. In the center is a large water-holding "bason." Penn, Washington, Jefferson, and other country gentlemen of that era had come to the conclusion that plants should not be shocked by cold water. Rain, being softer and warmer than ice-cold well water, was collected and then carried to the holding tank or "bason" in the garden, where the sun could warm it; only then was it dipped on to the plants. The "bason" looks like a well but actually is built on the ground; it stops at ground level when one looks down into it.

It is safe to assume that most colonial gardens were slightly less formal. Patterned, yes; clipped too, and used. But those who settled outside the more densely populated town areas were too busy maintaining life to trim complicated knot gardens.

In 1719 the Boston *Gazette* advertised "fresh garden seed of all sorts" from London and shortly afterward another commercial seed company was established in Philadelphia. Seed catalogs were beginning to appear on the scene. Robert Furber's catalog of 1732 is considered to be the first; showing flowers for twelve months, the engravings are much studied, reproduced, and used on the walls of today's homes. Gardens grew along with the seed companies.

A ten-acre public garden was established in Savannah, Georgia, in 1733, to study new agricultural methods. Mulberries (in the hope of starting a silk industry in this country), peaches, figs, coffee, cotton, bamboo, and many herbs were planted and observed. Capers, limes, olives, Alpine strawberries, fruit trees from France, and grapes were introduced in Charleston, South Carolina, to grow and to study. Gardens were burgeoning with new materials, those collected in the wild and those imported from abroad. Commercial nurseries appeared by mid-eighteenth century.

The Philadelphia Society for Promoting Agriculture was organized in 1785 and, in the same year, the South Carolina Society for Promoting and Improving Agriculture and Other Rural Concerns was soon followed by other famous horticultural societies still in existence in Massachusetts, Pennsylvania, and New York. They were primarily concerned at that time with farms and utilitarian gardens. Gardening for pleasure was a century away.

Seed catalogs, public gardens, horticultural societies — the pace of gardening in eighteenth-century America quickened. By 1776 available plant lists included almost all the ornamental plants in Europe in addition to those found amid the superabundance of this country.

Grandmother's "yard patch" was growing larger, blossoming into an old-fashioned flower garden. Still flourishing near the house, it was crowding out the herbs and vegetables because of her love of color. She took joy in sweet william, a bearded pink grown in colonial gardens for fragrance; foxglove, sweet rocket, and lunaria, self-sowing biennials; calendula and Johnny-jump-ups; many varieties of old-fashioned roses; and tawny day lilies, since then escaped from gardens and now growing wild along roadsides for everyone to enjoy in July.

As hybrids and imported materials flowed into commerce, gardens became more colorful, less formal. By late in the century perennials and shrubbery were planted extensively for beauty, providing accents for the many homes being built, and the herb garden, of considerably less importance to the household, was reduced in size. By 1850 Amos Bronson Alcott notes in an essay that gardens of herbs were becoming less frequent. Commerce and medicine were coming into their golden age; the usefulness of plants was beginning to be taken for granted.

THE KITCHEN GARDEN

> ". . . at Mount Vernon, Seat of Gen. Geo. Washing-
> ton in Virginia. An elegant kitchen and fruit garden
> containing 0.92 acres."

A trip to Mt. Vernon is a trip back into the time when the kitchen garden with its abundance of herbs and vegetables was a necessary fact of life. Here was grown all that was useful, in-deed essential, to man—to flavor foods, to give pleasurable fra-grance, to restore good health.

President Washington's instructions were explicit. "Tell the gardener," he wrote, "I shall expect everything that a garden ought to produce, in the most ample manner." According to Washington's personal correspondence, almost two hundred herbs and vegetables are listed as having been in the gardens, many of which are grown there today.

On Washington's birthday all visitors who come are admitted free to grounds and mansion. It makes a meaningful pilgrimage for families of children off from school for the day. I spent a good part of my allotted time in the kitchen and herb garden, while our children explored the coach house and stables.

The kitchen gardens are maintained in true colonial style with formal symmetry, containing only such flowers, vines, trees, herbs, shrubs, and berries as were common in Virginia during Washington's lifetime.

Beds are most carefully laid out, with orderly brick walks and crosswalks making a delightful pattern plus easy accessibility. Main alleyways are edged with cordons of pear or apple, fruit trees grown on low rails about a foot high—a handsome effect.

Included in the plan are great water cisterns, sizable cold frames, and, at opposite corners, the toolhouse and the neces-sary house. The whole is enclosed by a high brick wall on which grow espaliered fruit trees, with ony two gates for the entire 0.92 acres within.

Laid out in a pattern of great beauty to make evening strolls through the garden pleasurable as well as all the work accessible, the plot produced "in the most ample manner" enough for the needs of the ninety persons who lived at Mt. Vernon in 1786.

Fat mats of thyme, luscious edgings of lavender, thick borders of hyssop and santolina attest to great and needed harvests. Chicory, which we think of as a common roadside weed, was carefully cultivated. The young shoots are excellent greens and the roots were roasted for a hot coffeelike beverage.

As it is stated in the plan of the garden, "the several kinds of fruit tree, roots, pulse and herbs now grown are to be found named in the garden records of the general, or in lists which he

THE *MOUNT VERNON KITCHEN GARDEN* was restored in *nineteen Hundred and thirty six* in a Manner true to the Time of GENERAL WASHINGTON. The General had brought the Garden to the Present *Size* and *Shape* just one Hundred and fifty Years earlier and in his Writings, frequently referred to it. At the Time the *Restoration* was undertaken, no Trace remained of the original Patterns of Beds and Paths.

In evolving the new Design, the *Books* which the General owned and used, and the work *Accounts* which he kept, were carefully studied. In the Books were found Plans of Gardens with precise *Directions* for the laying out of the Ground and for the Culture of the Plantings. From the General's Writings came the *Names* of most of the Things which are grown.

All of the *Plants* now to be seen in the Garden were familiar to the eighteenth century Gardener. The *Amounts* of each which are planted are in *Proportion* to the Requirements of a Household such as the General maintained. A Supply of Water is kept in the different Parts of the Garden in "Basons . . . where it may be exposed to the open Air and Sun, that it may be soften'd thereby; for such Water as is taken out of Wells, Etc. just as it is used, is by no Means proper for any Sort of Plants."

The Kitchen Garden of Mount Vernon,
The Design of an Elegant Kitchen and

Grapes

Spearmint

Lima Bean

Fly

Primrose

French Marigold

Cherry

Beet and Carrot

Iris

Ivy-Leaved

Scale of feet

The several kinds of Fruit Tree, Roots, Pulse and Herbs now grown are to be foun

Designed by Morley Jeffers Williams, Director of Research and Restoration for the Mount Vernon Ladies' Association

t of Gen.ʲ Geo.ᵉ Washington *in* Virginia
arden Containing 0.92 Acres

Sage

Globe Artichoke

52
54
51
53
56
59
61
55
57
60
31 Glaucous Fumitory

Grape Hyacinth

Snowdrop Anemony

Pear

18
21
24
28
30
20
27
29
17
23
26
19
22
25

Pea

Chicory or Succory

Cabbage

Reflexed Daffodil

Strawberry

Pink

Jonquil

Saffron

Pepper

Celery

Potato

Natalia Utman '37

KITCHEN GARDEN PLANTING LIST
Mount Vernon, Virginia

BED
NO.

1 Apple and Pear Wall Trees (Strawberries)
2 Head Lettuce * Eggplant (Lavender)
3 Summer Onions * Beets * Summer Lettuce (Germander)
4 Artichokes (Nasturtiums)
5 Summer Lettuce * Turnips * Spinach (Germander)
6 Summer Lettuce * Turnips * Spinach (Germander)
7 Summer Onions * Beets * Summer Lettuce (Germander)
8 Head Lettuce * Eggplant (Lavender)
9 Apricot Wall Trees (Strawberries)
10 Peach Wall Trees (Lettuce)
11 Thyme (Lavender)
12 Thyme (Lavender)
13 Cabbage * Bush Lima Beans * Spinach (Rosemary)
14 Cauliflower * Carrots and Radishes * Winter Onions (Rosemary)
15 Cauliflower * Carrots and Radishes * Winter Onions (Rosemary)
16 Cabbage * Bush Lima Beans * Spinach (Rosemary)
17 Head Lettuce * Bush Beans * Kale (Thyme)
18 Head Lettuce * Bush Beans * Kale (Thyme)
19 Mint (Oregano)
20 Parsley (Lavender)
21 Mint (Oregano)
22 Fig Wall Trees
23 Carrots and Radishes * Okra (Thyme)
24 Parsnips (Thyme)
25 Fig Wall Trees
26 Sweet Fennel (Dill)
27 Peas * Cucumbers * Cauliflower (Lavender)
28 Potatoes * Summer Squash * Red Cabbage (Lavender)
29 Fig Wall Trees

BED
NO.

30 Beets * Spinach * Summer Lettuce (Parsley)
31 Fig Wall Trees
32 Sweet Basil (Rue)
33 Bush Beans * Endive (Chives)
34 Lily-of-the-Valley
35 Head Lettuce * Sweet Potatoes (Tarragon)
36 Head Lettuce * Sweet Potatoes (Tarragon)
37 Lavender Cotton (Dwarf Boxwood)
38 Broccoli * Summer Lettuce * Beets (Hyssop)
39 Horseradish (Dwarf Boxwood)
40 Currants (Mint)
41 Gooseberries
42 Strawberries (Thyme)
43 Strawberries (Thyme)
44 Strawberries (Thyme)
45 Strawberries (Thyme)
46 Lavender Cotton (Dwarf Boxwood)
47 Broccoli * Summer Lettuce * Beets (Hyssop)
48 Horseradish (Dwarf Boxwood)
49 Peas * Bush Lima Beans * Spinach (Sweet Marjoram)
50 Spinach * Summer Lettuce * Beets (Rosemary)
51 Peas * Potatoes (Thyme)
52 Peas * Potatoes (Thyme)
53 Peas * Summer Lettuce * Broccoli (Sweet Marjoram)
54 Spinach * Summer Lettuce * Turnips (Rosemary)
55 Salsify (Lavender Cotton)
56 Swiss Chard (Lavender Cotton)
57 Potatoes * Peas (Lemon Balm)
58 Tomatoes (Sage)
59 Sweet Peppers, Tabasco Peppers (Sage)
60 Asparagus (Lemon Balm)
61 Asparagus (Lemon Balm)

NOTE: * indicates "followed by"; border shown in parentheses.

is known to have used." These are the herbs and vegetables shown on the plan:

Apple	Fig	Salsify
Apricot	Gooseberries	Spinach
Artichokes	Head lettuce	Strawberries
Asparagus	Horseradish	Summer lettuce
Beets	Lavender	Summer onions
Bush beans	Mint	Sweet basil
Broccoli	Parsley	Sweet peppers
Cabbage	Parsnips	Swiss chard
Carrots	Peach	Thyme
Cauliflower	Peas	Tomato
Currants	Potato	

The Mt. Vernon Ladies' Association, who so wisely purchased this historical property, are fanatically dedicated to keeping the plantation as it was when Washington lived there. Therefore the gardens are not made to look showy with modern hybrids as is sometimes done at restorations. The ladies also, in their wisdom, sell the seeds gathered from the general's garden. It is an excellent opportunity for visitors to acquire herbs and other plants typical of an eighteenth-century kitchen garden, done up in handsome green packets. The garden is still producing, for them, "in the most ample manner."

I treasure my living souvenirs of our family's visit to Mt. Vernon. From seed, I have Washington's hyssop and tansy and rue; a healthy well-rooted cutting of the general's box has also been added to our herb garden.

THE BEE GARDEN

The honey bee has always accompanied man on his territorial expansions. It is man's most important insect, invaluable to his economy. The earliest colonists were well aware of this.

Over eighty-five percent of all plants, including trees, fruits, and grains, require insect pollination, a task well suited to the industrious, prolific, honey-gathering bee. For the sake of more productive gardening, the honey bee was brought from the Old World in the seventeenth century and, it is recorded, taken by clipper ship to California in 1853 and from there to Oregon.

Photo, by Richard H. Altenburg, courtesy of the author

A view of the author's garden, with her bee skep in the background. Lemon balm, garlic chives, germander, and monarda are all planted here.

Some feel that the honey bee was brought to this country by the Vikings because of their fondness for fermented honey in the form of mead. However, since there is no evidence of their doing so, let's stick with the records.

One of the primary purposes of the herb garden was the encouragement of bees. Honey was a natural sugar for the colonies, an essential sweet; beeswax provided candles and many other household necessities; the bees were needed to pollinate orchards and other crops.

Beehives were made of straw, elevated in the center of the garden, covered for winter protection. Although straw bee skeps such as this are no longer used by the keepers of bees, they are attractive additions to today's herb gardens. Handwoven exact reproductions of such antique bee skeps are sometimes available from basket weavers at craft fairs.

Honey was an important medication as well as an ingredient to sweeten medicines. According to Dr. Jarvis, in his best-selling book entitled *Folk Medicine*, honey was and is a fact of life in Vermont, used for both quick energy and as a sedative, to stop coughs, as a laxative, to end bed-wetting, to allay hay fever, to control muscle cramps, and to soothe burns. Who could want for more from any one food—a veritable home medicine chest?

If one is stung by a bee while he is working in the herb garden, there are several simple, old-fashioned remedies: tobacco juice, for one; also onion juice; crushed savory leaves; a bit of moist mud; baking soda. In all probability a dab of honey would work too.

Herbs to be planted in the bee garden—those which specifically attract and keep bees—are lemon balm, thyme (all varieties, including lemon), winter and summer savory, teucrium, garlic chives, monarda, lavenders, hyssop, pineapple mint, catnip, clove-gillyflowers or pinks, cowslips, all mints, borage, anise-hyssop, lilies, roses, sage, southernwood, and rosemary; also, butterfly weed, wood betony, marjorams, sweet basil, coriander, dill, and angelica.

Monarda is a "must." This plant was discovered in America by the earliest settlers and named after Monardés, a Spanish physician and botanist, in 1656. There are many varieties, such as *Monarda didyma,* the scarlet-flowered one, sometimes called bee balm; *Monarda fistulosa,* the wild bergamot with purple flowers, tinged lavender; and *Monarda punctata* with spotted flowers, called horsemint.

Flourishing in vast fields in New York state, New England, and through the West, the native monardas go by many names, such as bee balm, fragrant balm, bergamot, Oswego tea. This last name was given it by the early pioneers who were introduced to it by the Oswego Indians. Used as a tea, it is one with rather an untamed, minty taste. After the taxed tea from England was dumped into Boston harbor, the revolutionaries turned to native teas, bee balm being one of the most popular.

And then there's lemon balm *(Melissa officinalis)* which must be included in every bee garden. The very name melissa means bee! Uses of this fragrant lemon-scented herb are limited only by one's imagination. It can occupy a semishaded position in the bee garden. Fistfuls of lemon balm were sometimes rubbed inside new hives to keep swarms from leaving.

An outstanding bee herb, thyme, should be grown in the bee garden in all its forms, creeping and upright, culinary and lemon. Thyme, it was said, "yielded most and best honie."

There are, of course, many other bee plants such as clover and

A Heritage of Herbs

locust tree blossoms for which the South is justly famous, but these are field and woods plants for the surrounding areas and not necessarily included in the bee garden. The bees will find them.

THE APOTHECARY'S GARDEN

"... potent and parable medicines" — Cotton Mather.

Behind the eighteenth-century apothecary's shop or the doctor's office was found a garden of medicinal plants. Called "the physick garden," the dispensers of medicines grew their herbs, gathered, prepared, and administered them as they were needed.

The practice of medicine in the colonies was not confined to licensed graduates of accredited medical schools. Physicians were not in abundant supply and, depending upon his locality and his means, the colonist turned to the person with a "physick garden" and the knowledge necessary to dispense the plants — perhaps an apprentice to an apothecary or physician, a recently arrived colonist with a family background in herbs and a new supply of "simples" to draw upon, or to a friendly Indian who searched the woods for his medicine.

Not everyone knew all the "secrets" possessed by these plants, nor was everyone endowed with the gift necessary to identify, extract, and administer the healing herb. The doctor, apothecary, or local herbalist, frequently the "wise woman" of the area, treasured this knowledge and revealed it only to the immediate household or to those who could pay for it in money, goods, or services. Her "wort-cunning" was a valuable commodity, a legacy to be carefully recorded and passed on to selected successors.

The "physick garden" was reminiscent of old monastery gardens, crammed with those herbs necessary to the treatment of the sick. Called "simples," these medicinal plants possessed a single virtue that was used as a simple remedy.

In many colonial homes the gathering and preparation of simples was the housewife's single most important task, rarely entrusted to children or servants. She pursued these activities, compounding her medicinal concoctions for the family needs, storing them in carefully labeled jars, bottles, or crocks for later use.

88

Colonial Herb Gardens

Photo, by Robert S. Halvey, courtesy of Pennsylvania Hospital

Park of "the Physick Garden" of Pennsylvania Hospital, in Philadelphia, where trillium, used during the eighteenth century to induce fever, is being planted.

Doctors and apothecaries grew their "physical plants" near their shops; hermits and Indians brought needed medicinal plants, gathered in the wild, to the towns for sale and trade; itinerant peddlers traveled the colonies selling and exchanging the herbs grown best in each area. Spring, summer, and fall were periods to harvest essential herbs and botanicals from the family garden, the apothecary's garden, or adjacent wilderness areas. Life depended upon such activity.

To use the herbs medicinally took a knowledge and skill that was a rare gift, a combination of plant and people physiology. One needed to understand the inner workings of both. Doctors were expected to be versed in botany, at least concerning the "physical plants."

It was always important to use the correct variety of the herb, grown under proper conditions of soil and climate, harvested at exactly the right point in its life cycle, and dried with utmost care. The dosage and preparation were equally vital considerations.

Besides all this, there was — and still is — the strong possibility that the herb that worked well for one person or complaint would have no effect whatsoever on a different person with the same complaint.

That certain plants are still efficacious cannot be denied. We must all agree that digitalis is now, as it has been for centuries, among the most effective heart medication that we have. Similarly, the poppy has given man a long list of the most powerful painkillers known in the history of medicine. These are only two of the more than two hundred plants listed in our modern *materia medica,* half of the herbs known and used by Hippocrates centuries before the discovery of America. We don't always know how the plant works, but we do know that it works. Many of these herbs, the poppy and digitalis particularly, are drug plants, dangerous in the hands of all but the most competent physicians.

Herbs were used for protection as well as in the treatment of disease — the forerunner of preventive medicine. Doctors carried canes with perforated heads filled with herbs to sniff, to ward off the dangers of "venomous air." The "hex doctors" of Pennsylvania Dutch areas prepared charms against all sorts of evils and ills, mostly from herbs along with other mysterious ingredients. The Indians had their medicine man with wild rituals and strong medicines to drive away the demons of illness.

Witches and the strange potions they brewed for their terrifying craft were taken seriously, and herbs were used just as seriously to strike back at this evil practice. The most powerful of these was angelica; carrying the root was considered an effective charm. Another favorite protection was Saint-John's-wort, which was gathered on the eve of the Feast of St. John (June 23rd) and hung in bunches for the rest of the year to protect the entire household. Saint-John's-wort has since escaped the gardens of those earliest settlers and can be gathered easily along our roadsides.

Some of the herbs associated with witchcraft and other such deviltry include wolfsbane, tobacco, opium from the poppy, cinquefoil, saffron, poplar leaves, henbane, hemlock (the poisonous herb, not the evergreen), mandrake, and nightshade. No innocent list of homely simples this, but, rather, dangerous, sometimes deadly drugs, to be treated with the greatest respect in anyone's hands, witch or no.

A "physick garden" adapted from the eighteenth century could encompass such plants, both drugs and simple herbs, as those mentioned. There are countless more from the official listing of two hundred in today's *materia medica*. From such a garden the doctor, the apothecary or his apprentice, the housewife, or the local herbalist would dispense endless medications.

Madonna lily petals were preserved in alcohol and used as a poultice; wild ginger, growing in moist, shaded woods, was an aromatic rootstock used by the Indians for indigestion; lily-of-the-valley root was powdered and administered for heart conditions; and rhubarb, used as an early spring vegetable, was also medicinal, for the root is laxative.

Other Indian herbs, their secrets revealed to the settlers, are bistort, for snakebite; Indian pipes, which made a lotion for weak eyes; tobacco, used on wounds and smoked in peace pipes; lady's slipper root tea, a sedative and also for use on poison-ivy rash; and pipsissewa, the roots and leaves made into a tonic tea.

The Indian word *kinnikinnick* describes a mixture of dried herbs and bark smoked by the pioneers, who were taught by the Indians of the Ohio River valley and Great Lakes regions. The native plants used in this smoking mixture were: red bearberry *(Arctostaphylos uva-ursi)*, silky cornel *(Cornus amomum)*, red osier dogwood *(Cornus stolonifera)*, and sumac *(Rhus virens or R. microphylla)*.

Here also were dispensed dandelion bitters for the liver; wintergreen tea for rheumatism; peppermint for indigestion and heartburn; saffron as a tea for jaundice; sage tea against colds; wild native columbine seeds to be brewed into a tisane for headaches; and feverfew — its very name its purpose — to abate fevers.

Herbs that grew in the fields were gathered and preserved, later dispensed as medicines. Fields, meadows, woods, and bogs, everywhere; leaves, trees, roots, barks, seeds, and flowers, everything — all were used as teas, liniments, potions, ointments, poultices, and liquors.

Thomas Jefferson listed these plants as grown to be used medicinally in his household: senna, arsmart, lobelia, castor bean, angel's-trumpet (datura), mallow, ipecac, marshmallow, butterfly weed, Virginia snakeroot, valerian, ginseng, angelica, and rattlesnake root.

Some of the others you might like to consider for your "garden of simples" are violets, hepatica, Christmas rose, feverfew, hen and chickens, flax, betony, comfrey, rose mallow, hore-hound, wormwood, lungwort, aloe, elecampane, pennyroyal, coltsfoot, boneset, and rosemary.

Large clumps of tansy and rue and southernwood would be cultivated here, each in a space sufficient to its importance as a medicine. Yarrow would be planted nearby. Believed to increase the potency of medicinal plants, it "strengthens their virtues."

A medicinal herb garden such as this, well labeled, will excite more interest than any other kind you could plant. The list of herbs to be considered is almost endless, limited only by the size of your plot and your endurance.

No beautifully designed, clipped, and controlled pleasure garden is this one; rather, in this place a working collection of those plants necessary to the treatment of man and his infirmities in another time.

THE DYER'S GARDEN

In November 1789, George Washington records in his diary that on a visit to Portsmouth, New Hampshire, he was given an ear and stalk of red "dyeing corn" and materials of various colors that had been dyed with it. He was very impressed.

There is considerable controversy among those who know much about plant dyes as to what kind of "corn" this was. Or was it corn at all, or simply a generic reference to some other grain? Also, what part was used—stalk, kernels, silk, root, or leaves?

The "dyeing corn" may be lost in antiquity but the important part of the story is the reference to the matter of dyeing with plants, the impact of new colors created from another dyestuff. The economic importance of botanicals used in this way was vital to the commercial development of this country.

Herbs necessary to the dye trade were gathered in the wild or grown as a crop, whichever was feasible. Shearing sheep for wool, spinning linen threads from unbleached flax, were labors made joyous by the prospect of its transformation with bright colorful dyes. Most of the herbs were available in generous quantities in the surrounding wilderness areas, generous enough so that American herbs used in the dye industry soon became one of our main exports.

Raw materials, primarily wool, were first mordanted—a process of making the wool accept the color so that it is a dye and not a stain by actually changing the molecular bonding structure of the wool. Then it was further processed in dye baths made from available herbs. The same dye bath could produce different results, depending upon the mordant of the number of times the dye itself had been used.

Mordants available to the colonial housewife included alum (a natural earth deposit), urine, salt, green vitriol, and blue vitriol. The inventive colonists also made mordants from rusted iron, old nails, and filings from the forge, some of which produced grayed shades which they called "saddening." Cream of tartar, acquired by gathering the crystals from the edge of wine kegs, was used as a brightener during the mordant process. To add a bit of tin to brighten the color was called "blooming."

They liked large iron or untinned copper kettles for dyeing because of the effect of the metal upon the color. Sometimes several colors were achieved from one dye bath by adding different mordants or additional dyes. An unsatisfactory color could be redyed a darker color. The mordant was used hot and the general instructions were to "handle until the color pleases."

According to *The New England Courant* of 1721, Ben Franklin's older brother James had a printing shop in Boston where he printed calico fabric of "lovely and durable colors," so says his advertisement. The colors were achieved with plant dyes just as, some two hundred years later, juniper berries produced the khaki color of uniforms worn during World War I.

The present interest in dyeing with natural materials is alive and well. Craft shows, museums, and apartments are dripping with hanks of raw materials and dye pots full of various botanicals. Today's enthusiasm for this old-time occupation is shared by many and with good reason.

Natural dyes last infinitely longer than chemical colors, mellowing and blending into each other at the same rate, an aging process that makes them more beautiful and valuable with the passage of time. Although we don't necessarily understand why it happens, this long-lasting quality with compatible natural colors produces a product as much in demand today as in years past.

A general rule for dyeing woolen yarns is a pound of the botanical to a pound of wool. Prepare the dye by boiling the plant in water covered, strained, and set aside for later use. With few exceptions, almost all dye plants are used fresh. In today's twentieth-century kitchens we can freeze such a mixture and keep it almost indefinitely.

Mordant a pound of wool with four ounces of alum in three to four gallons of water, simmered an hour and then kept in the water to cool for overnight. Remove and hang to dry.

Then simmer the mordanted woolens in the dye bath, to which three to four gallons of water have been added. Simmer and stir with a long wooden spoon until a good color is achieved. Rinse, squeeze gently, and dry in a dark warm place. Variations in color are frequently due to the place where the herb grew, when it was harvested, the variety of the plant, or the quality of the water used during the dye process.

Color in a dye pot becomes a living experience, an exciting, creative relationship between plant and material and the dyer. Experimentation can yield surprising results; it's best to keep careful records of recipes, successful or otherwise. Note also when and where the dye plant was acquired.

Yellow colors are the easiest to achieve. True greens and purples are the most difficult and among the most desirable; success with these is cause for elation. Blue is easy with indigo, a plant dye once sold by itinerant peddlers. There was a brief experiment in the production of indigo in this country long ago and it proved that it can be grown here in the South; however, most indigo comes from India, then as now.

Woad is always listed with blue dyes because of its ancient usage as a blue dye plant. It is rarely used today because of its dreadful odor while fermenting—impossible to live with, especially if one has any close neighbors. By all means, grow this biennial plant in your dyer's herb garden because of its past economic importance in this regard and because of the luminous golden flowers that will greet you very early in the spring. It is a pretty herb, one that will self-sow itself where it wants to grow.

A dyer's garden, unless it is a demonstration plot planted as a part of a restoration project or farm museum, is usually highly naturalistic. The poundages required for dyeing materials can be gathered from fields, roadsides, or woods. Black walnut trees, a hedge of junipers, elderberry or barberry bushes are not easily confined to small patterned herb gardens. Goldenrod, a valuable dye plant, will soon populate a field. On the other hand, a sampling of each of these along with a few plants of indigo or woad would be an eminently suitable dyer's garden for show-and-tell purposes.

THE COLOR	THE HERBS
Red and Rose	Madder; root of lady's-bedstraw; pokeberry (not a fast color); bloodroot (too precious as a wild flower to gather and use today); the root of rue.
Orange	Onion skins; coreopsis; madder and any yellow dye, mixed.
Yellow	Osage orange root; greater celandine; barberry root; goldenrod flowers; apple twigs; milkweed, to all parts of which a bit of clear ammonia is added; tansy; peach, pear, birch, or poplar leaves; broom sedge, fresh or picked in June (one of the few that can be dried and used all year); lamb's quarters; lady's-bedstraw tops; rhododendron or laurel leaves; sassafras; black oak (inner bark); goldenseal.
Blue	Indigo (formerly sold by peddlers; available today commercially); woad.
Blue Green	Yellow top-dyed with indigo.
Green	Indigo top-dyed with a strong yellow.
Moss Green	Horsetail in copper; black-eyed Susan blossoms; Queen Anne's lace, saddened; barberry root in copper; most yellows, with the addition of iron, saddened.
Violet and Purple	Logwood, peachwood (brazilwood), both from Central America; elderberry; some lichens.

Beige	Juniper berries; onion skins; and many unsuccessful dye baths.
Brown	Black walnuts; butternut bark; many tree barks; lichens.
Gray	Sumac; blackberry shoots, saddened; rhododendron leaves, saddened.
Black	Yellow flag iris root; indigo and black walnut, dark and strong.

THE SENTIMENTAL GARDEN

"There is a language, 'little known,'
Lovers claim it as their own.
Its symbols smile upon the land,
Wrought by Nature's wonderous hand;
And in their silent beauty speak,
Of life and joy, to those who seek
For Love Divine and sunny hours
In the language of the flowers."
—J.S.H., from *The Language
of Flowers*, London, 1875.

Herbs were used in so many ways down through the centuries that people began to endow them with even greater attributes. Because of their versatility of uses and effect upon people, the mysterious ways in which they could heal, their magical properties, real or imagined, herbs became a form of communication, an expression of love, victory, or sentiment suitable to all occasions, proper to religious ceremonies and affairs of state. Herbs became symbolic.

In days long past, man had no need that a plant could not satisfy, directly or indirectly. Food, housing, clothing, medicines, and pleasure—the eternal usefulness of plants was always the answer. Man could not seem to exhaust their powers, nor could he endow them with enough mysteries. They became truly magic.

Victorian gardens spoke eloquently. Fragrant small bouquets called tussie-mussies were a favorite floral tribute; flowers held hidden messages but none spoke with more charm or authority than the herbs. Nosegays became the love letters of the day; every

Photo courtesy of the Tyler Arboretum

The herb wall in the Fragrant Garden for the Blind at the John J. Tyler Arboretum, in Lima, Pennsylvania.

diminutive bunch was searched for hidden meanings. The message was love.

Symbolism . . . magic . . . love—for those who do not wish to experiment with the many practical uses of herbs but would like to grow them simply because "their silent beauty speak," there is yet another way to enjoy these remarkable little plants in your garden. Cultivate a garden of sentiment.

Today we can adapt this particular form of herbal nostalgia to many occasions. Tiny meaningful bouquets from your garden of sentiment lend their messages to anniversaries, bon voyage, initiation ceremonies, graduation, or the advent of a new neighbor—those special times that crop up when selecting a gift becomes a dilemma. Pick a bouquet with a message—a charming presentation.

Perhaps you would like to call it an "olitory"—the old-fashioned word for a fragrant garden. To grow a pleasure garden, select plants from this old list of flowers and herbs with their symbolisms and sentiments.

Allyssum	Worth beyond beauty
Amaryllis	Pride
Apple blossom	Preference
Bay laurel	Glory, victory
Burnet	A merry heart
Chamomile	Energy in adversity
Clover, red	Industry
Cress	Stability
Foxglove	Sincerity
Lavender	Luck
Lemon verbena	Enchantment
Mint	Cheerfulness
Rose	Love
Rosemary	Remembrance
Rue	Repentance
Sage	Health, domestic tranquility
Thyme	Courage
Violet	Humility

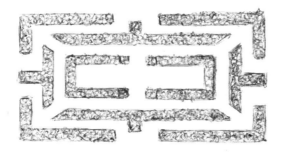

Heritage of Herb Gardening and Recipes

THE ROSE

Small rose plants, tended during the long voyage from the Old World as carefully as the children, were brought to this country from home gardens. Frequently they were the first root to be set down in new wild territory as pioneers headed west. It was the link with a known way of life, a vital possession to be tended, nurtured, always making a home of a strange new garden plot, there to become a part of the history of the people and the land. The adornment of roses in the garden became "hereditary in the new land."

Spanish gardens in Saint Augustine were small and enclosed, graced by the rose, which grew so well at home. The English colony of Virginia included roses almost from the beginning. Gardens were established quickly because of the mild climate and tobacco prosperity.

The many weeks of ocean travel followed by stern winters precluded rose-growing for those first arrivals in New England until the early 1700s, when the rose was their first choice of a plant for beauty and utility.

"Its history, its romance, its usefulness as an agency of human happiness" is well known; fragrance and flavor, rose water, sachets, jellies, syrups, medicines, rose hips for tarts, and potpourri for rose jars are a few old-time favorite rose recipes. The shrub roses, with fragrant petals and abundant oversized hips (the seedpods), yielded a generous harvest suitable to these uses.

Roses, legacy of the Roman legions, were brought here by the English, Spanish, and French, thence on across the country by the pioneer woman in her saddlebags or planted in an old worn-out shoe, a cherished gift, symbol of one home in establishing roots in a new one. These transported treasures were given such nostalgic names as Allegheny Rose or Red Rose from Kansas.

Old roses of this period in our garden history, those suitable to restoration gardens or for background borders for herb gardens, are of four main types: Gallica, Centifolia, Damask, and Alba, as well as their many hybrids from natural or man-made crosses between types. These are the oldest roses still sometimes found marking the site of a once-loved home, an old log cabin, abandoned manse, or tumbledown farmhouse, where only the remnant of a garden persists to tell the rugged story.

The names of some of these old varieties suitable to a restoration project might be helpful to those involved in such work, personal or community. The old Red Gallica *(Rose gallica officinalis)* sometimes called "The Apothecary's Rose," distinguished by its large red flowers and golden stamens, was brought to England by the Romans and thence, much later, to New England in colonial times. It is a prized addition to medicinal gardens, the petals being distilled into syrup of roses and used for soothing medications, especially for hysteria, and was also made into ointments. It was known as the rose of the House of Lancaster.

The rose of the House of York was *Rosa alba,* or the white rose, double, sweet-scented, the most ancient rose grown in England. Red Centifolia is the cabbage rose beloved of painters, along with its nostalgic sport the Moss Rose. *Rosa mundi* was grown throughout the colonies; its mixed red and white blooms were popular in nosegays. *Rosa damascena* was the rose brought to France by the Crusaders and its famous sport, *Rosa damescena versicolor,* the York and Lancaster Rose, sometimes red, sometimes white, sometimes both. The Sweetbrier or Eglantine mentioned by Shakespeare, noted for its fragrant leaves, was planted along walks "to perfume the circumambient air to a considerable distance." In addition to these there were the single Musk Rose; the Cinnamon Rose; the Burnet Rose, Pimprinella; *Rosa Canina,* the Dog Rose; and *Rosa Villosa,* the Great Apple Rose, famous for its large hips.

Any such listing of historical colonial roses must also embrace our native varieties, *Rosa carolina, Rosa lucida,* and *Rosa palustris,* which were taken back to England to be grown and much admired.

These, then, were the ancient roses, now at home on yet another continent, the most durable, hardy, vigorous-growing of all the roses. They flower profusely in June, sometimes remontantly during the summer and fall, resembling the double silk roses piled high on an elegant lady's hat.

Colonial ladies gathered bouquets of roses, wild or cultivated, together with other flowers, fresh or dried, and placed them in their homes by the window so the breezes wafted their perfume into the house. Rose petals were gathered in abundance during June to be distilled and bottled for use as a skin refresher, to dry for potpourri. It was said roses in cookery "maketh a man merry and joyful."

Sweet-scented old-fashioned roses massed in pewter or china and joined by herbs are at home anywhere you place them. Roses should be added to the June diet, giving grace and color to spring salad greens and adding unexpected flavor to ordinary fare. For a touch of the eighteenth century in the twentieth, add some pretty pink rose petals to your pancake batter or puddings, freeze your nicest rosebuds in cubes for special drinks, or use them as a garnish for a festive cake. They can also be baked on top of cherries in a pie—an old, old secret. Use only the reddest petals for this.

To make a quick and easy potpourri, mix the dried rosebuds and petals with basil, thyme, mint, lavender, and other fragrant herbs; add such spices as ground cinnamon, cloves, allspice, and some dried lemon peel, ground orris root, and a few drops of your favorite perfume to make it fragrant. Age in a tightly closed container from four to eight weeks, stirring it occasionally. Then transfer it to pretty jars. Open it to use it; close it to restore the fragrance.

There are many splendid historical roses worthy of note in any herb garden, most of them being vigorous growers of enormous proportions in need of great space and thus suitable only to large gardens or backgrounds. My first choice for our small herb garden is a newer little hybrid called The Fairy. A nostalgic pink-colored polyantha, The Fairy yields an abundance of small roses blooming nonstop from mid-June to mid-November with less care than any other rose I know.

Not especially prone to diseases or attractive to insects, rarely in need of weeding, the glossy-leaved shrub adds a great deal to the herb garden. It can be clipped in early spring to retain the size desired. And the flowers! They are always a charming addition to every herbal bunch, especially nosegays. We could not create our endless chain of tussie-mussies without the prolific, beautiful, sentimental little roses produced by The Fairy. They also dry well for use in herb wreaths, which we make with silvery artemesias, sage, and santolina combined with the little double pink roses.

TO ROOT OLD ROSES

Since very small plants were the only possible way to transport roses that grow so vigorously, frequently to enormous size, they had to be rooted in preparation for the trip. Space aboard ship or covered wagon was too limited to give more than what was absolutely necessary to any plant.

Simple layering was and is the easiest method. Take a long flowering cane, remove the flower, and make a partial slit on the underside about a foot in from the tip; apply rooting powder to the slit. Then bend it down to a well-prepared section of earth next to the mother bush; cover the slit, leaving several inches of the tip above ground. Anchor it with a rock or forked branch over the buried portion and wait until the tip shows signs of new growth, usually the following spring, when the new rosebush may be severed from the mother bush and planted elsewhere.

To start from cuttings, use a side shoot, preferably a heel

cutting taken by grasping the branch at its base and pulling downward to leave a bit of the main stem attached. My gardening mother called these "slips." Do not take a tip cutting, as they are reluctant to flower. The days from June to August are the best times, when the new soft growth has begun to mature. Dip the bottom of the stem into a rooting hormone, shake off the excess, and firmly plunge the cutting into a well-prepared bed of very good soil, almost potting soil, well aerated by sand or vermiculite, in a spot shaded by a shrub. Allow several leaves and the tip to remain aboveground. Water well; then cover each cutting with a large glass jar and it will root in a month or so. If it is taken late in the year, allow it to remain under the jar until spring.

A collection of old roses is a hobby for some people. Abandoned farmhouses, ancient cemeteries, hedgerows will yield cuttings of unexpected variety. Plants are also available from specialists in historic roses.

ROSE PETAL SANDWICHES

    1 large 8 oz. pkg. cream cheese
    3 T. rose water
    12 slices thin white bread, crusts removed
    6 unsprayed red, red roses ("Blaze" will do)

Mix the cream cheese and rose water into a smooth spread; divide it evenly among the slices of bread, spreading it carefully on all pieces, to the edge. Place the petals from each rose on each of six slices of bread, pressing them well down into the cheese. Cover and firm. Cut the sandwiches with a kitchen shears by cutting in half, then each half into fourths. Place them on a pretty plate with the cut side up, showing the bright-red petals. Garnish with several of the same roses. These sandwiches are delicious and have been the hit of every party at which they were served.

ROSE SYRUP

    1 c. sugar
    1 c. water
    1 c. fragrant red rose petals

Boil the sugar and water for 15 min., add the roses, from which all green or white parts have been removed from the base, and steep until cooled. Strain (or not), bottle, and use on ice cream, pancakes, waffles.

ROSE BUTTER

"Wash petals and put them in a stone jar, sprinkling them with fine salt. Next day gather some more and repeat until the jar is almost filled. Keep the jar well covered at all times with a lid and also wrapped in coarse cloth. When you plan to make rice pudding or cake, weigh the butter you intend using and put it in the jar on top of the rose petals overnight. By the time you take it out, it will have absorbed a very fine rose flavor, superior to that of rose water. Rose petals may be kept in this manner for a year—or until the rose blooms again." This recipe is over a hundred years old.

ROSE SKIN CREAM

⅓ c. rose water
⅓ c. glycerin
⅓ c. lemon juice

Mix ingredients together, shaking vigorously. Pour into a pretty bottle; then use on face, neck, and hands as often as you choose.

ROSE TOBACCO

Using old-fashioned red rose petals and maple or soft brown sugar, alternate flowers and sugar in a crock. Cover with a weight, such as a rock. Allow the layers time to fuse into a brown gummy confection, which is served and eaten in small pieces. This is a recipe for a very old confection.

TO MAKE ROSE WATER

Gather about a pound of fresh rose petals from your most fragrant roses. Precise housekeepers of long ago used only the fragrant Damask roses for the making of rose water. Petals must be carefully washed, preferably unsprayed. Fill a teakettle half full of water; strew the petals thickly over the surface. Close kettle and set over low heat. Attach a rubber hose to the spout of the kettle and place the other end in a glass jar on the floor. Part of the rubber hose is so arranged that it can be submerged in a pan of cold water. The essence of the rose petals will be extracted by the heat, which will vaporize and be carried off with the steam generated by the water. The vapors on passing through that part of the rubber hose which is underwater are condensed and run into the glass jar in the form of rose water. (From *Rose Recipes*, by Jean Gordon. Used by permission.)

ROSE HIPS, THE FRUIT OF THE ROSE

Gathering rose hips is one of the more satisfying joys of the fall season. It is a bonus one receives for growing old-fashioned roses. The round red seedpods of rosebushes, large or small, new hybrids or old-fashioned, are entirely edible, a desirable addition to the year's harvest.

The writer of one old herbal says, "Children with great delight eat the berries thereof when they are ripe and make chains and other pretty geegaws of the fruit; cooks and gentlewomen make tarts and suchlike dishes for pleasure." "Delight" and "pleasure" and "pretty," he says—adjectives well applicable to rose hips; add to these "delicious," "available," and "healthy" for an even truer word picture.

Since rose hips have more vitamin C than oranges, tomatoes, and lemons combined—a cup of rose hips being equal to fifty oranges—why not cultivate a closer friendship with this delicious available fruit?

You can buy rose-hip tea, of course. It even comes in tea bags. However, if you are gathering your own, clean the hips, then chop or crush them in a blender, air-dry them before storing in a tight container until you use them. To make the tea, use about ½ teaspoon of the crushed hips to a cup of boiling water; steep five minutes until the color is bright pink. Add sugar, honey, or lemon if you like, and by all means try it with cloves and cinnamon-stick stirrers.

Northern Europeans have known about the delectable edibility of rose hips for centuries and have many choice recipes for the fruit of the rose. Take a pail to the garden or nearest hedgerow and gather the scarlet fruits after they have been frosted and are completely ripe. Then dry and store them, or use them fresh, to make tea or the following recipes for soup or jam, all of which have a pretty rosy color, most attractive.

ROSE-HIP SOUP

    2 c. rose hips
    2 c. water
    ½ c. sugar
    2 T. cornstarch
    ½ c. white wine

Cover the rose hips with the water and cook 2 hours or until they are tender; then add sugar. Thicken with cornstarch; boil briskly 3 min., stirring constantly. Add white wine just before serving. If served cold, garnish with whipped cream. Serve it hot with lemon slices.

ROSE-HIP JAM

Wash 1 qt. rose hips well and remove the green stems and calyx. Then simmer in a kettle with a cup of water until they are tender. Put through a food mill or blender, add sugar in an equal amount, simmer until thick (about 10 min.), and seal in sterilized jars. This is delicious on ice cream.

GRANDMOTHER'S POUND CAKE
(with rose filling and frosting)

     1 lb. sugar
     1 lb. butter
    12 small or 10 large eggs
     1 lb. all-purpose flour
     ½ t. baking powder
     ⅓ c. rose water

Cream sugar and butter about 10 min. until very light and fluffy. Add egg yolks one at a time and cream well. Sift flour twice; then add about ½ c. at a time to sugar, butter, and egg mixture, folding in with a spoon. Beat whites until they form peaks; then fold them in. Add the baking powder and the rose water. Grease two 9"x5" loaf pans. Line the pans with greased brown paper and pour in the mixture. Bake in 375° oven for 15 min.; then reduce heat to 325° and finish baking for 45 min. more. Leave cake in pan for ½ hour to cool before removing to place on a rack.

ROSE AND ALMOND FILLING
3 T. butter
2 c. confectioner's sugar
2 T. rose water
¾ c. chopped toasted almonds

Cream butter; gradually add confectioner's sugar and rose water; beat until creamy. Add chopped almonds. Use as a filling for above cakes, which have been cut in half.

ROSE-FLAVORED BUTTER FROSTING
½ c. butter
1 lb. sifted confectioner's sugar
4 T. or 5 T. rose water
Dash of salt

Blend all ingredients; beat vigorously until smooth and creamy. Ice above cakes. Decorate with real roses and serve proudly.

DOTTY O'BRIEN'S ROSE WINE
4 qts. red rose petals
4 qts. boiling water
¾ of a large cake of yeast
4 lbs. granulated sugar

Using a five-gallon crock, put the petals in the crock, with sugar on top. Pour the 4 qts. of boiling water over it and let it stand until it is lukewarm. Then add the dissolved yeast cake and stir. Let it stand exactly six weeks. Strain and let it stand one month. Then put it into a jug and cap it. IMPORTANT: use exact timing.

If you use a cork, set the jug on its side to keep the cork wet. This makes three gallons of the most delicious wine you have ever tasted. The petals from unsprayed old-fashioned climbers, such as Blaze, are best; they are easily gathered in quantity and have the most flavor.

BOXWOOD

Boxwood was the stuff of which memories were made. To remind the colonists of home and, coincidentally, to deter small animals from their kitchen gardens, the colonists planted boxwood hedges as soon as homes were established and gardens laid out. The hedge was always a handy place for the Virginia housewife to lay out her linens, especially newly woven flax, to dry and bleach. Homespun could thus be kept high and flat, alternately exposed to dew and sunshine until it turned a silvery white. She also probably gathered boxwood, along with American holly and the traditional ivy, to decorate her home at Christmas.

Brought from England, box *(Buxus sempervirens)* is durable and slow-growing, well suited to large or small gardens. Many original colonial boxwood plantings are still preserved and tended, as at Mt. Vernon and Monticello. The variety *suffruticosa,* a permanent small-leaved evergreen, has been used for centuries as an edging, eminently suited for knot gardens.

John Parkinson, seventeenth-century herbalist, when writing of the various plants to be used in knots, says of box, "Above all other herbs, I recommend to you, to set out any reasonable thick set, will be easily cut and formed into any fashion one will. The nature thereof . . . is to grow slowly, and will not, in a long time, rise to any height. This I commend and hold to be the best and surest herb to abide fair and green in all the bitter storms of sharpest winter and all the great heats and droughts of summer."

Farther north than the Maryland and Virginia areas, where it grows superbly, box must be planted in protected areas. Other varieties of box can be substituted; however, because they grow at a much faster rate, more clipping will be required. Following one particularly dry summer and bitter winter, we had a disastrous taste of winterkill in our hedge of old box here in south-central Pennsylvania. Recovery took two years.

In the event boxwood, English or the more hardy sorts, is out of the question for your herb garden, substitute yew or holly or arborvitae for hedging. Washington, in his instructions to his gardeners, suggested hedges "for ornament and for use." His recommendations were honey locust from seed, the hawthorns, cedars, or any evergreen. Holly hedge was popular in colonial gardens to separate kitchen garden from flower garden.

Boxwood hedges are clipped in March before new growth begins or later in August. To increase the plantings, cuttings are easily struck at almost any time from late spring through summer. Use short lengths (about 6") of semihard wood, not soft new growth. Scrape the end slightly with a pocket knife to expose more surface for rooting, dip it into a rooting powder, and tuck it firmly in a good mixture of coarse sand, vermiculite, and some peatmoss. Tamp the cuttings firmly in place, water well, and, after draining, cover the container with clear plastic. Keep it shaded and watch for new growth which signifies rooting activity. If all conditions are right, you should have at least eighty percent success.

The small hedge in our herb garden is taken almost entirely from rooted layered cuttings cut away from the bottom sides of very old boxwood shrubs. This is the easiest, quickest, and most economical way to acquire additional boxwood hedging.

Boxwood is without peer for topiaries, accents to the formal eighteenth-century pleasure garden or to the herb garden. A basic form, once achieved, must be kept trimmed constantly. Clip it any time of the year to keep your plant in the form you wish. It doesn't hurt the plant. Quite the contrary, it will grow more vigorously and reward you with highly desirable densely compact growth, becoming more beautiful and valuable with the years.

ESPALIERS AND TOPIARIES

Since an herb garden is a quiet garden, not so flamboyant as one set with flowered bedding plants, it is desirable to accent the design with such features as espaliered shrubs, topiary trees, well-clipped hedges.

A garden set against a house or outbuilding may benefit most by shrubs or trees espaliered against the background wall, adding pattern and height during twelve months of the year. A form is constructed of wires, pipes, or wooden posts and, by continual clipping and tying, the plant is trained to conform to all the upright and cross-pieces. It is also possible to screw strong hooks directly into the wall to support the plant. Train the espalier to the pattern decided upon in advance and keep it well controlled by clipping constantly.

We have as a background to our herb garden three apple trees espaliered on a wooden frame against the garage. The training is done entirely by removal of unwanted growth and by tying. There couldn't be an easier way of giving our small city garden great definition, not to mention the spring blossoms and a few fall fruits. Fruit trees, especially crab apples, are appropriate to use. Also, pyracantha, grapes, wisteria, cotoneaster, climbing hydrangea, and ivy lend themselves to this type of espalier training.

You can, of course, develop a freestanding espalier or purchase one already trained into a pattern. It will take constant vigilance and great horticultural skill to maintain an espalier without a framework, but it can be done.

Topiaries are achieved by pruning to remove all unwanted growth and by clipping to maintain a pattern, usually a rounded ball, pyramid, spiral, or cone on a standard—the main stem. Start to form your standard by removing all bottom branches. This forces upward growth of the tree. Begin clipping the top to sculpt the shape you desire. Removal of all bottom branches along the trunk and close shearing of the top is a process that sometimes takes years. When the desired size and shape is achieved, constant vigilance is required to keep off unwanted branches and the compact top growth in shape. It will not hurt the plant to do all this cutting and it can be done safely at any time of the year. I repeat, it will not hurt the plant.

Privet, boxwood, ligustrum in the South, pyramidal juniper, hollies, and yew are a few of the possibilities that will tolerate the constant clipping necessary to maintain a topiary. Bay, myrtle, and rosemary are prime subjects for herbal topiaries. These need to be grown in tubs in cold climates so that they can be brought indoors in winter. Tubs also lend them great mobility; they can be placed to give distinction to the landscape.

To train a garden feature into either geometric or animal shapes take a good eye and considerable patience. A razor-sharp pruning tool also helps. If wiring is necessary, use #8 galvanized iron wire, adjusting it as required. Heavy wire frames have been used to create the many topiary animals displayed at the Disney parks, a shortcut to the tedious shaping that requires years of trimming and shearing to achieve a good, dense freestanding sculpture.

Animal shapes were popular during the extravagant Victorian era, when gardeners skilled in plant sculpture were available and tastes were both sentimental and lavish. But earlier, in colonial days, there was little time or inclination toward such fanciful horticultural exercises. And so where there were topiaries, as on the large estates of Virginia and some Southern plantations, the shapes were primarily geometric.

Traditional to an eighteenth-century herb garden, well worth the time and effort required, an espalier or topiary makes a charming addition to today's garden, appropriate to the quiet intimacy of the small herb plot.

THE PRUDENT WIFE

> Strength and honour are her clothing; and she shall rejoice in time to come. She openeth her mouth with wisdom; and in her tongue is the law of kindness. She looketh well to the ways of her household, and eateth not the bread of idleness. Her children arise up, and call her blessed; her husband also, and he praiseth her. — Prov. 31:25-28

Recipes for medicines, ointments, cosmetics, distilled waters, and all such concoctions were the charge of the colonial housewife. This was done in the cottage kitchen, or in a summer kitchen attached to the rear of the house, or in a special room a slight distance away. Sometimes in the South the lady of the plantation had a place similar to a seventeenth-century European stillroom for such preparations, which she referred to as her "office." Here she made her potions and filled her basket before going to visit or see the sick. Martha Washington concocted some medicines in her bedroom as well as in the kitchen and, it is recorded by a sick guest, George himself once came through the door, carrying a candle, bearing tea to ease his cough.

Photo, by Donald F. Eaton, courtesy of Old Sturbridge Village

An historically costumed interpreter at Old Sturbridge Village Herb Garden, Sturbridge, Massachusetts, reaches toward a clump of woundwort or lamb's ear.

It is not so long ago that summer kitchens existed next to most country homes in parts of Pennsylvania and throughout the colonies. They were separate small buildings, sometimes connected to the main house by a passageway, and practical, to keep excess heat out of the home on hot summer days. Here, not in the main house kitchen, they hung the herbs awaiting winter use. There was also a fireplace, crocks, iron vats, copper kettles, a mortar and pestle, perhaps a small still, and necessary equipment.

The industrious housewife distilled her herbs and flowers, turning them into precious oils and salves, extracts of the herbs, cordials, and lotions according to ancient recipes handed down from generation to generation. These were the medicines she worked with in the face of dread fevers and terrible illnesses. Her recipes were carefully written down along with comments and instructions and then to be passed on through the family. Such small notebooks are now rare museum pieces.

In those early days herbs were not grown as ornaments. In America hardship was the rule; herb-growing was a serious business, vital to health, food, good housekeeping. Cosmetics, fragrance, dyestuffs, insect repellents, and first aid were just a few of the ways to use them. Dependency on these simple plants occurs again and again in their records.

Dispensed by the skilled colonial housewife to family, servants, and neighbors, the washes, liniments, poultices, extracts, and home remedies of the day were her most vital responsibility. Grinding powders, distilling extracts, preparing oils and liquors essential to the household; soap, perfumes, lotions; yes, jams and jellies, were all part of the summer kitchen labors.

Eventually the apothecary took over these chores, making and marketing the herbal preparations as well as imported medicines. He, or the local village "yarb woman," could devise a herbal dose upon request. Williamsburg, with a population of a thousand, supported six apothecaries.

These, then, are some of the recipes vital to the health and well-being of every member of the household. You might like to try some, either using ingredients gathered in your own kitchen garden or those which may be purchased. We include, also, some fragrant recipes for pleasure—washing water, cologne, and bath drops.

LICORICE COUGH SYRUP

1 t. linseed
1 oz. licorice root
¼ lb. raisins
2 qts. soft water
Boil above down to 1 qt. and strain.
Add ¼ lb. brown sugar and 1 T. vinegar.
Drink before going to bed for a troublesome cough.

Licorice roots were chewed as a natural toothbrush and breath refresher. They were also a sweet treat. The hard, dried roots yield their sweetness reluctantly; chew very determinedly and you will be rewarded with a taste sweeter than sugar.

HERBAL SALVE

Melt lard, available at supermarkets, or lanolin, available at drug stores. Add such herbal ingredients as aloe, comfrey, golden seal, slippery elm, and simmer slowly. Strain off the herbs and jar the salve. May be melted and simmered again with fresh herbs for greater strength.

STRAWBERRY FACIAL

Rub cut strawberries over the face to whiten the skin and remove sunburn.

WRINKLES MIXTURE

1 oz. white wax
2 oz. strained honey
2 oz. juice of lily bulbs

Melt and mix. Apply daily.

COSMETIC VINEGAR

An aromatic vinegar to be used as a beauty aid, for the complexion or the hair, or to saturate a sponge and be placed in a vinaigrette (worn on a chain) "to sniff unto" in case of an attack of the vapors. For the same effect today's lady would soak a small towel to lay on her forehead while she was resting.

> 1 qt. white vinegar
> 1 oz. Roman wormwood
> 1 oz. rue
> 1 oz. rosemary
> 1 oz. lavender
> 1 oz. mint
> cloves and cinnamon, a pinch of each

Combine the herbs and spices into a large glass or enamel container and pour over the well-heated vinegar. Let it stand 2 to 3 weeks, in the sun, shaking occasionally; then strain and bottle to use as a soothing calming lotion, or to sell at bazaars as "toilette Vinegar."

RINSE FOR DARK HAIR

Sage, boiled in an iron kettle, was used on the hair to keep dark hair dark. Still used today, it works as a natural dye.

RINSE FOR LIGHT HAIR

Pour a quart of boiling water over ¼ c. of camomile blossoms. Steep 20 minutes, strain, and use as a hair rinse; dry the hair in the sun if possible. It will give it golden highlights.

1897 COLOGNE

This recipe, written by hand in a small notebook and dated, was found by a friend in his father's effects. It is a delightful gentleman's cologne which we prefer to use as a bath oil.

½ oz. oil of bergamot
¼ oz. oil of lemon
½ oz. oil of orange
½ oz. oil of lavender
½ oz. neroli (orange blossom)
1 qt. good rubbing alcohol (or vodka)
Combine and shake bottle several times a day for
three weeks.

WINTERGREEN RUB

1 dram oil of wintergreen
1 pint witch hazel
Combine and bottle. Label. A rub for sore muscles.

Witch hazel was great-great-grandmother's beauty secret. She
distilled her own astringent by gathering bark, twigs, and leaves
in the fall when the oils were at their peak quality. The Indians
poured hot water over the fragrant leaves to brew a soothing
tonic tea. The wilted hot leaves were also used as a simple poultice
for bruises and sprains, soothing the sting of insect bites or quiet-
ing a sunburn.

HERBAL LOVE BATH

7 c. lavender
6 c. rosemary
5 c. rose petals
4 c. lovage
3 c. lemon verbena leaves
1 c. each thyme, mint, sage, marjoram, orris

Mix all the dried herbs thoroughly and keep in a tightly lidded
can. To use, place ¼ cup in a muslin square and tie securely.
We put these up in pink and red calico, tying with red wool. Boil
the bath ball in 1 qt. water for 10 min. Add to hot bath water
and scrub yourself with the little love bath ball. Think serene
thoughts and luxuriate!

SCENTED BATH LOTION

Using a good quality rubbing alcohol or witch hazel, add mints, lemon balm, rosemary, and lavender, both leaves and flowers. Steep for two weeks in full sun, stirring gently every day or so. It will turn a beautiful soft herby green. Strain, label, use as a fragrant rub after your bath.

ELDER FLOWER BEAUTY BAG

Gather and dry all the elder flowers you can. Make these beauty bags of small terry cloth washrags, folded into a triangle and stitched on the machine with a small opening. Stuff the bag and use it to wash the hands and face, to soften and whiten the skin.

Perfumed baths were popular in colonial times—a luxury reserved for those who had the servants or stamina to carry the water to and from the tub. It was also considered an important remedial measure for certain maladies, in which case herbs for the bath water were prescribed.

RECIPES FOR LIBERTY TEA PARTIES

On December 16, 1773, American patriots boarded three ships at anchor in the Boston harbor and threw overboard 342 chests of black tea bearing the damnable British tax—the act that triggered our American Revolution.

Now we can commemorate their daring and spirit, the remarkable leadership shown by those brave revolutionaries, toasting their dedication and zealous spirit of independence by drinking and serving herb teas. It's an occasion to fire the imagination of all in attendance at any such gathering.

After the dramatic events that began our historic struggle for freedom, the colonists were exhorted in their newspapers not to drink tea from England which "endangers our Liberties and drains our Country of so many thousands of Pounds a year" but, instead, to use "our own American Plants, many of which may be found pleasant to the taste, and very salutary, according to our various constitutions . . ." (from *The Virginia Gazette* of Williamsburg, 1774).

Anytime is the right time for a tea party and any day the right occasion. If you are looking for a new way to entertain your friends and neighbors, Girl Scout Troop, garden club, church circle, or members of a working committee, you really should try having a "liberty tea party."

Although people in European countries have always enjoyed drinking herb teas, we, unfortunately, are inclined to think of them as something medicinal and not something to be enjoyed.

As with any party, you can do as little as you like or as much as time permits. It's up to you whether a simple spur-of-the-moment party is possible or whether there is time for days of planning and preparation. Whichever you choose to try, you will be delighted with the magical results.

Herb teas are made the same as any other tea — by steeping the leaves, dried or fresh. Using one teaspoon per cup (½ t. of the dried herb), pour fresh water brought to a rollicking boil over the herb. Steep as long as necessary for a good flavor, remembering that too long steeping could produce a bitter taste. Most herb teas are a golden-green brew, fragrant and delicious, good for you and your state of mind. They lead to quiet thoughts.

Seeds such as dill, anise, or fennel need to be slightly bruised to release their fine fragrance. Roots and barks like sassafras and birch are best boiled for good results. Some of the teas require sweetening, accomplished by adding honey, rock candy, or molasses.

This list, by no means complete, will give an idea of the herb teas available — used in the early days of our land and suitable for a tea party.

Spicebush	Wintergreen	Sage
Bergamot	Ambrosia	Sweet fern
Orange mint	Pennyroyal	Peppermint
Spearmint	New Jersey tea	Lemon balm
Costmary	Linden flowers	Camomile
Cinquefoil	Red clover	Comfrey
Sassafras	Elder flowers	Marjoram
Thyme	Red rose leaves	Fennel
Parsley	Sage	Sweet gum twigs
Strawberry leaves	Rosemary	Rose hips
Raspberry leaves	Violets	Lemon verbena
Catnip	Dill	Fragrant goldenrod

Not all of these teas will be to your liking; many can be gathered in the wild or in your garden and tried in gentle potions, sweetened if you wish, with lemon or cream added. It is also possible to combine two or more of the herbs into a satisfying brew, as they did in colonial times.

To carry out the herbal theme throughout your entire party, send herb and spice invitations, informal notes with pressed herbs applied. Or simply enclose a sprig of fresh mint with the necessary information on when and where. Decorations should also help reflect the mood of the party; a simple bunch of fragrant herbs gathered from your garden is charmingly sufficient. Little pots of herb plants are an appealing centerpiece and make delightful favors as well.

Put on your herbal thinking cap when you plan your menu and be sure to include mint cookies, herbal dips, candied flowers, rose geranium sugar, rosemary jelly with hot biscuits, and similar tasty tidbits. All the recipes and more are in this book. A recipe card for each guest with one of the recipes served at your tea is a commendable way to thank each guest for coming. Perhaps it will inspire her to have a Liberty Tea Party of her own.

If you are not certain as to the tastes of your guests, it can be fun to serve different kinds of teas such as mint, rose hips, linden, camomile, lemon verbena, and fennel. All of these, and more, come in tea bags, which can be piled in a basket next to the teapot of boiling water. A herb tea-tasting party such as this will initiate endless chatter among your guests.

Here are some additional recipes to help you plan.

MRS. DUNLAP'S MINT TEA

6 large cans apple juice, heated
1 box (24) mint tea bags
1 c. lemon juice
5 sticks of cinnamon
1 pt. of honey, or to taste
1 T. mint extract, or to taste

Steep tea bags in 3 qts. boiling water; strain; then add the heated apple juice and all other ingredients. Serve this tea hot with cinnamon stick stirrers. Makes 2½ gal.

SPICED TEA

½ lb. orange pekoe tea
4 t. grated orange peel
2 t. grated lemon peel
2 3" sticks cinnamon, crushed
¼ c. whole cloves
1 t. grated nutmeg
1 c. slivered candied orange peel.

Combine all ingredients and mix thoroughly; store in a closed tea canister. This is a very old recipe which is easy to make. Use ½ t. to a cup of boiling water. It can be used in your Liberty Tea Party menu and small containers of it given as favors too. The tea keeps well in tightly covered jars.

FRESH LEMON BALM TEA

20 sprigs of fresh lemon balm
4 T. honey
10 whole cloves
½ lemon, juice only

Pour a quart of boiling water over the herb, add other ingredients, and steep 10 min. Strain and serve the aromatic lemony brew.

LEMON VERBENA TEA

Depending upon the number of cups desired, use 1 t. of the dried leaves, slightly crushed, per cup of boiling water. Steep 7 min. and serve, sweetened with honey.

SASSAFRAS TEA

½ c. sassafras to 4 c. water. Boil 10 to 20 min. The bark may be used several times over. Drink hot or iced. This tonic tea, used since the time of the Indians, is truly delicious spiced with whole cloves and cinnamon bark.

FRESH MINT TEA CONCENTRATE

Gather a generous quantity of good black peppermint, spearmint, or applemint. Stuff a large china teapot with the well-washed leaves, pour over very briskly boiling water, and allow to steep for 20 min. When you serve it, dilute to taste with another separate pot of hot water. We like this tea with a thin slice of lemon or orange, finding no sweetening necessary. Suit yourself. The concentrate may be made in advance and in great quantity for a large gathering.

INDIAN LEMONADE

Gather red sumac berries in late summer or fall. Steep them in gently simmering water for ten minutes, strain through cloth, add honey and ice for a tart pink drink. Dried sumac berries are used in winter.

NEW JERSEY TEA

"In 1768 tea made from a plant* or shrub grown in Pearsontown about 20 miles from Portland, Maine, was served to a circle of ladies and gentlemen in Newbury Port, who pronounced it nearly, if not quite, its equal in flavor to genuine Bohe tea. So important a discovery claims attention, especially at this crisis. If we have the plant, nothing is wanted but the process of curing it into tea of our own manufacture." — *The Boston Gazette,* 1768.

RASPBERRY LEAF TEA

"We have known families in America to use Raspberry Leaf Tea instead of Oriental tea; and we have no doubt that if the young leaves of this plant were gathered and sent to China, or some other distant part, and thence returned to England bearing some strange and unfamiliar name, it would sell as well as any other tea, and prove much more wholesome in the end."
— *Botanic Guide to Health,* 1845.

---

*New Jersey Tea *(Ceanothus americanus).*

BICENTENNIAL TEA

   1 c. bergamot, leaves and petals if available·
   1 c. lemon balm
   1 c. pennyroyal
   2 c. mints (spearmint or peppermint or a combination)
   ½ c. fennel seeds
   ½ c. violet leaves and blossoms
   ¼ c. sassafras bark, cut fine

Mix all dried herbs, seeds, roots, and flowers thoroughly. Keep in tightly closed container. Use 1 t. per cup of boiling water, more or less as desired; steep 10 min. Do not use a metal pot. Sweeten with honey or lace with rum. Stir with a wooden spoon while steeping. This tea is a savory combination of the liberty teas gathered and used by the colonists during the Revolution; it is a palatable and tasty tea guaranteed to revive the Spirit of '76.

SUN-BREWED TEA

Before the days of pilot lights and electric ranges, the stove remained cold, the fireplace unlit for as long as possible on a hot summer's day. On any sunny day you can make your favorite tea by sun-brewing. Use tea bags in a glass jar of water if you wish. Or try this herbal blend.

   1 c. fresh peppermint leaves
   ½ c. lemon balm leaves
   1 T. rosemary tops
   3 sage leaves

Place all ingredients in a gallon glass jar or crock. Fill with fresh water. Put in full sun; move it as the light shifts; shake or stir occasionally. At the end of a long hard day, strain, add honey and enjoy a truly refreshing herbal blend, warm from the sun or iced. And think about the early settlers who did this during the summer.

OLD SETTLER'S TEA

Turtlebloom *(Chelone)*
Licorice root
Althaea
Fennel seed
Cheeseplant (Malva)
Rocky Mt. grape root
Bittersweet
Hops

This rather nebulous formula, with no amounts given, is of historical herbal interest. I don't know if the name refers to an old recipe or an old settler. If it was an old settler, it's because he drank this beneficial brew!

OSWEGO TEA

The herb (*Monarda didyma* or scarlet bee balm) should be gathered before it flowers for best flavor. Simmer the leaves, ½ t. to a cup of water, until desired strength is achieved — 5 to 10 min. A strong tea, it can be combined with other tea herbs and is usually served sweetened with honey. One of the red blossoms, gathered from roadside or garden, will flavor a pot of regular tea.

RECIPES FOR HERB COOKERY

We can be sure the great American tradition of recipe-swapping began on that first Thanksgiving Day, in 1621, when the ladies, as today, cooked endlessly, enough for the three-day feast. Chief Massasoit and his ninety braves joined the remaining small band of Pilgrims in their celebration of their first splendid harvest at "Plimouth Plantation," the best of all the harvests. Thanksgiving for health and home and harvest has since become an American tradition, now celebrated by proclamation.

The Indians brought five deer to roast and many turkeys, still accepted fare. That first Thanksgiving dinner menu featured pumpkins, beans, turnips, squash, corn, "sauqeutash," clams, oysters, codfish, seafowl, baked Indian whortleberry pudding, and all the bounties this land and their labors could provide. The feast was a welcome change from pease porridge, or the "good English pottage," or a kind of soup made of corn, strawberry leaves, and sassafras root.

Today any holiday is reason enough to get out favorite recipes, gather together friends and family to feast in the spirit of the same American tradition. Many recipes have been with us for hundreds of years and, with some slight variations through the passage of those years, are still much in use. Here is a compilation of recipes, old but updated, to add to your collection.

RABBIT DINNER

    1 rabbit, skinned and cut up in pieces
    ¼ c. oil
    ⅓ c. flour with salt and pepper
    1 bunch fresh rosemary (substitute 1 T. dried)
    2 cloves garlic, crushed
    ½ c. cooking sherry
    2 c. water

As the proverbial recipe starts, "first catch a rabbit." Rub the skinned rabbit vigorously with the rosemary, then coat with the flour and brown in oil. Remove rabbit; add all other ingredients (the dried rosemary is used here if substituted) to the oil, and boil to make a broth. Place rabbit in a casserole, pour the strained broth over it, bake covered in a 350° oven for an hour.

EASY PEANUT SOUP

Peanuts, much grown in colonial and present-day Virginia, are highlighted on the bill of fare when a local church holds its annual "Williamsburg Dinner" and serves this twentieth-century version of peanut soup.

    1 onion
    2 T. butter
    4 T. flour
    2 qts. chicken broth (may be canned)
    1 t. celery salt
    2 c. smooth peanut butter
    chopped peanuts

Brown the onion in the melted butter; then add the flour to make a roux. When smooth, blend in the chicken broth and simmer until it thickens. Add celery salt. Finally stir in the peanut butter (a shortcut from the old laborious method) until creamy. Serve hot with additional chopped peanuts as a garnish. It may also be served chilled.

SOUTHERN BAKED SQUASH

2 c. squash (or pumpkin)
½ c. milk
3 eggs
2 T. cornstarch
½ t. vanilla
½ t. nutmeg
½ t. salt
½ c. sugar
2 T. melted butter

Whip eggs lightly, add milk, blend into squash until smooth. Combine all ingredients. Bake in casserole at 350° for 45 min.

MOCK INDIAN PUDDING

½ loaf whole wheat bread
3½ c. milk
½ c. dark molasses
1 c. chopped sweet apple
1 c. suet, chopped fine
1 t. ginger
½ t. cinnamon
½ t. cloves

Arrange sliced bread, crusts removed, in a baking dish. Mix all remaining ingredients and pour over, reserving a cupful of liquid. Bake from two to three hours in slow oven, 250° stirring three times during the first hour of baking; then add remaining liquid. Stir and finish baking. Serve with custard, ice cream, or hard sauce.

HERBED HUSH PUPPIES

2 c. cornmeal
1 c. water
1 t. salt
3 T. fresh parsley and chives and thyme

Mix all ingredients and deep fry in hot fat. If dried herbs are used, substitute 1½ T.

BRUNSWICK STEW

1 chicken (or squirrel), cut in pieces
1 c. leftover ham cubes
6 tomatoes, chopped
1 pt. lima beans
2 c. corn
1 t. savory
1 T. parsley
1 t. basil
1 onion, minced
salt and pepper to taste

Stew all together until the meat is tender. Correct the seasonings to taste. May be thickened with cornstarch if desired. Always better the next day. Cubed potatoes and okra are optional additions.

CLAY-JACKETED TROUT

If you are fortunate enough to catch a fish where there is a bank of clay, try this old Indian method of fish cookery. Some of us who are gardening in clay can do the same at home with purchased fish. Knead a large ball of clay on a clean board, pat it out into an oblong an inch thick and place the trout in the center, wrapping it firmly in the clay. Parsley, thyme, fennel seed, and a touch of nutmeg may be added before sealing; or use just plain salt and butter. Cover the jacketed fish with glowing embers. In an hour or two the clay may be opened and the delectable dish served.

WEED SOUP

2 qts. weeds (Good-King-Henry, lamb's-quarters,
sorrel, nettles, plantain, et cetera)
5 c. water
2 c. potatoes, diced
3 minced onions
1 c. salt pork
2 egg yolks
herbs, salt, and pepper to taste

Wash the weeds, one or all in combination, thoroughly and boil
twice (except for garden sorrel if used); drain then throw away
the first cooking waters. Crisp the salt pork with the onions in a
large pan; add the chopped parboiled weeds, the potatoes, and
the 5 c. water. Season with salt and pepper and any herbs your
family enjoys (a pinch each of thyme, parsley, rosemary, and
tarragon is good); simmer until the potatoes are soft. Add the 2
lightly beaten egg yolks slowly at the end of cooking. Serve hot.

TURNIP SLAW

2 medium-sized turnips
¼ c. vinegar
⅓ c. sugar
½ c. oil
1 T. dill (seed or weed)
salt and pepper

Peel and grate the turnips. Combine the dressing and pour over,
mixing well. Chill until served.

HERB BUTTERED HOT BREAD

¼ lb. butter, softened
½ t. thyme
¼ t. summer savory
½ t. paprika
1 clove crushed garlic
1 loaf crusted bread, French or Italian

Mix the butter and herbs thoroughly. Remove the upper crust from round or oval loaf of bread, cut down to the lower crust in 1″ slices, open and spread the herb butter between each slice and on top. Wrap loosely in foil. Bake 15 min., 350° oven.

TOMATO KETCHUP

1 gal. tomatoes
4 T. salt
4 T. cloves
1 T. mace
1 T. cayenne
2 T. allspice
8 T. white mustard seeds
2 whole peppers, chopped
1 oz. garlic
1 pt. good vinegar

Combine all ingredients and boil away to nearly half. Strain. Bottle. Cork. —*Recipe dated 1875.*

MINTED GRAPES

1 lb. cluster of green grapes
½ c. sugar
½ t. ground cardamom
1 T. finely crushed dried mint
1 slightly beaten egg white

Cut the grapes into small clusters, individual portions. Dip into the egg white and set aside on waxed paper. Sprinkle with the combined sugar, cardamom, mint mixture, covering all sides of grapes. Refrigerate until needed to garnish a meat platter, cheese board, or fruit bowl.

OLD PROSPECTOR'S JERKY

Trappers and traders, mountain men and Indian scouts, those rugged individuals who traveled long distances on foot or wagon, subsisted on dried, salted strips of meat called "jerky," which they could carry in their pockets. Made from venison, buffalo, any wild game or beef, the meat is sliced paper thin, then boiled until it is no longer red. Marinate the meat strips overnight in water to cover to which you have added:

    1 T. salt
    1 T. onion powder
    1 T. garlic powder
    1 T. pepper
    1 T. chili powder

This pungent spice mixture may be as strong as you like. Individual recipes were developed according to the availability of seasonings, the taste and talents of the cook. They used seasonings galore. The next day remove the meat strips and drain. Place them on a cookie sheet and bake in slow oven, 250°, 2 to 4 hours until very dark, almost black, but till they will not crack when bent. In intensely hot climates this was done outdoors on hot rocks in full sun. Indians devised drying racks 3 or 4 feet above the campfire and smoked the meat continuously for a day or two. "Jerky" will keep indefinitely.

NATIVE AMERICAN BERRY BUCKLE

    ¾ c. sugar
    ¼ c. soft shortening
    1 egg
    ½ c. milk
    2 c. flour
    2 t. baking powder
    ½ t. salt
    1 pint blueberries, cranberries, strawberries,
      or raspberries

Mix the sugar, shortening, and egg thoroughly; then stir in milk. Sift together the dry ingredients and stir in. Finally blend in the native American berries of your choice. Spread batter in a greased, floured pan 13″x9″x2″ and top with the following crumb mixture, then bake at 375° for 30 to 35 min. CRUMBS: 1½ c. sugar, 1 c. flour, ½ c. softened butter, 1 T. cinnamon, ½ t. cloves, ½ t. allspice, ½ t. nutmeg, ¼ t. mace.

PUMPKIN SOUP

The pumpkins grown here in colonial days were something to marvel at, prodigious in size, in great quantity, and of good taste. They were cut into pieces, strung, hung, and dried for year-around use. It was the pumpkin that kept the first colonists from "Wante or famine." Traditionally incorporated into the Thanksgiving feast, usually as pie, this soup is adapted from a very old recipe.

Cook the pumpkin flesh (no skin or seeds) until soft enough to puree through a sieve. Combine 2 c. pumpkin, 3 T. butter, 1 t. sugar, 1 t. salt, and ¼ t. white pepper. Cook gently for 10 min.; then slowly add 3 c. hot milk and return to simmer. Serve hot with crusty hot bread.

PUMPKIN SPICE CAKE

    ½ c. shortening
    1⅓ c. sugar
    2 eggs
    1 c. canned pumpkin
    ⅔ c. buttermilk or sour milk
    1¾ c. sifted flour
    2 t. baking powder
    1 t. soda
    1 t. salt
    2 t. cinnamon
    ½ t. nutmeg
    ¼ t. allspice
    ¼ t. ginger

Cream the shortening and sugar until it is fluffy; add the eggs one at a time, beating well after each. Combine the pumpkin and milk. Sift the dried ingredients together. Add the liquid and dried ingredients alternately to the creamed mixture, beating well after each addition. Bake in greased floured 13″x9″x2″ pan, at 350°, 40 to 45 min. Cool. Frost if desired.

'Tis said the honey bee and the dog have accompanied man on all his travels. I believe you could add to this herbs and the apple tree. Every settler's cottage had, as soon as possible, a producing apple tree. Appropriate to the kitchen garden where there is room, shade-tolerant herbs will thrive under or near the apple tree. A tree to adorn a cabin with its flowers in spring, to give shade in summer, and bless the pioneer with health-giving fruit in fall and winter, the apple flourished throughout the land.

It inspired a real live folk hero, "Johnny Appleseed." John Chapman by name, "the Appleseed Man" was born in September 1774, a Revolutionary War baby. He carried his leather bag of apple seeds wherever his travels as an itinerant preacher took him. Planted along the roads, on farms, in open places throughout Ohio, Western Pennsylvania, and Indiana, his apple trees, mostly Rambos, were enjoyed and appreciated for generations afterward. It is said he also carried herbs, distributing them to homesteaders' wives in exchange for his necessities.

He was so convinced of the efficacy of dog fennel, similar to boneset, in the treatment of malaria that he planted it everywhere; now it grows as an abundant weed up and down the Ohio River Valley, its presence attributed to his zeal, outliving his apple trees.

The apple was a year-round staple; a family would put by 40 to 50 barrels of cider, cold cellars were filled with the fruit, damaged fruits were cut and dried for storage, available then until the following year's harvest. In September, when the apples are coming in, toast the man who became the legend with apple cider, hot or cold, or apple mead. Serve it with apple pie, apple cake, or good apple butter on hot, homemade bread.

JOHNNY APPLESEED FROSTED CIDER

1 pt. lemon sherbet
1 qt. cold sweet cider

Mix together in a punch bowl, stirring until well frosted. Serve immediately, dusted with freshly grated nutmeg and use whole cinnamon stick stirrers.

HOT MULLED CIDER

1 qt. water
3 c. sugar
6 whole allspice
6 whole cloves
1 3" stick cinnamon, broken
1 orange, cut in pieces
1 lemon, sliced

Boil together for 10 minutes. Remove from heat. Cool 1 hour. Strain. Add to it 2 gal. apple cider. Heat together and serve hot. Garnish with orange slices stuck with whole cloves.

APPLE MEAD

½ apple cider
½ honey

Mix and allow to ferment. Skim and bottle.

YUMMY APPLE CAKE

2 c. sugar
pinch salt
2 t. soda
2 t. cinnamon
½ c. oil
2 eggs
4 c. diced apples
1 t. vanilla
1 c. nuts
2 c. flour

Mix sugar, salt, soda, and cinnamon in a large bowl. Add oil and blend thoroughly. Add eggs; beat well. Then add apples, nuts, vanilla. Mix well and then add the flour last, beating gradually until it is smooth. Bake at 350°, in a 9"x13"x2" pan, 40 to 45 min. until it seems done. (This can vary with the moisture content of the apples.) It is best mixed by hand; the electric mixer mashes the apples.

FROSTING

    4 T. flour
    1 c. milk
    ¼ lb. soft butter
    ½ c. shortening
    1 c. granulated sugar
    1 t. vanilla

Mix the flour and milk; cook, stirring constantly until thick. Let mixture cool. Cream together the butter, shortening, and sugar; add vanilla and cream again. Combine both mixtures and beat until smooth.

EIGHTEENTH-CENTURY MUSTARD

Mustard was most vital to the health and feeding of the settlers. It made foods palatable, especially salted and dried meats, as well as aiding in the digestion of same. It is easy to make your own mustard; once you have done so, you will never want to buy it again. There are many recipes, but we are not hampering your imagination with any specific amounts. Rather, this is designed to aid you to develop your own personal mustard, depending upon the ingredients available to you and to your family's palate.

You will need ground mustard flour to start. If you wish a mild English style, add vinegar. A pungent mustard is made with white wine. A sharp hot mustard is accomplished by adding water. If you really like it so hot it curls your toes, do it the Chinese way and mix with beer. This may be thinned with mayonnaise or milk if desired (not salad dressing.)

Here is your choice of herbs; select as many as you like, safe in the knowledge that the mustard flavor will always predominate. Be adventurous!

Horseradish	Lovage	Tarragon
Basil	Turmeric	Parsley
Sage	Rosemary	Dill
Oregano	Marjoram	Tabasco
Paprika	Chili	Curry
Garlic	Cumin	Mustard herb (the tops)
Onion	Allspice	Nutmeg
Chervil	Cinnamon	Savory
Cloves	Thyme	Chives

Mix the spices, herbs, and mustard flour thoroughly before adding the liquid. Add sufficient to make a smooth paste; then allow it to stand until well blended. Bottle. Mix in small batches for greater pungency. This mustard keeps indefinitely.

One last word of advice: Write down your recipe as you devise it. If it's a winner, your family and friends will want you to make more of it. You will want it also for gifts and to contribute to your favorite bazaar.

> "Why should any man that has a garden buy mustard? Why should he want the English to send him out, in a bottle, and sell him, for a quarter of a dollar, less and worse mustard then he can raise in his garden for a penny?" — *The American Gardener,* Boston, 1842.

EQUIVALENTS

In all recipes, standard measurements are used, i.e., 1 t. is one teaspoon; 1 T. is one tablespoon; 3 teaspoons equals 1 tablespoon. 2 cups equals 1 pint, et cetera. There should be no problem with these terms.

TEN RULES FOR USING HERBS IN COOKERY

1. Cut your herbs in the morning before the sun gets hot, while flavor is at its peak; dry or freeze the surplus not used in the day's recipe, labeling for later use in cooking.
2. In any recipe, consider using herbs as a salt or sugar substitute.
3. Snip the herbs with a kitchen scissors.
4. At first, try herbs one kind at a time; later they may be combined for more adventurous cookery.

5. Use ¼ t. of the dried herb at any time in any recipe as a start. Increase the amount in subsequent uses of the same recipe. Note your corrections.
6. Use twice as much or more of the fresh herb as dried.
7. ¼ t. powdered herb = ½ t. dried herb = 1 T. chopped fresh herb.
8. ½ t. garlic salt = 1 clove of garlic (omit or adjust salt in recipe).
9. 1 t. dried dill seed = 1 head fresh dill.
10. 1 T. onion flakes = 1 medium raw onion.

Today's Public
Herb Gardens

IF A PICTURE is worth more than ten thousand words, then surely seeing the real thing must be worth much more. I cannot encourage the visiting of herb gardens enough. It is a practical way to learn about plants and their cultivation. In response to inquiries to the fifty states, I have many public gardens to list for your exploration. Visit those closest to you and plan to take in some of the others as your vacation plans permit. Garden plans, features, design ideas, methods of cultivation, and the many kinds of plants to include in your own herb garden are only a few of the relevant ideas for you to capture at public herb gardens and then bring back to your own. The gardens are listed alphabetically by state.

CALIFORNIA

Arcadia: The Herb Garden of the Los Angeles State and County Arboretum, 301 North Baldwin Avenue, is open daily except Christmas from 9 a.m. to 5 p.m. The garden covers 1.2 acres and contains about 300 different herbs, mainly medicinal, fragrant, and kitchen. Included is a Braille Scented Terrace. Admission is free.

Sacramento: A fragrant garden is planted at Encina High School, 1400 Bell Street, with a large inventory of plants for fragrance; many tropical ones.

San Francisco: Strybing Arboretum, in Golden Gate Park, features a "Garden of Fragrance"—a half-acre garden with wide, smooth paths edged with stones from an ancient monastery. The plants are marked with braille signs for visually handicapped persons.

Photo courtesy of Denver Botanic Gardens

In the formal herb garden at the Denver Botanic Gardens the brick paths create the knots in this unusual design.

137

COLORADO

Denver: Denver Botanic Garden, 1005 York Street, is open to the public from 10 a.m. to 5 p.m., free. Sponsored by the Denver Botanic Gardens Guild, the garden features a statue by Louisa May Arps and a sundial surrounded with a variety of herbs, fragrant and culinary, teas—all that will grow in the Colorado area. Future plans call for an arbor and a gazebo.

Denver: The Eugene Field House, at 715 South Franklin Street, has a herb garden that is open to the public at no charge.

Denver: The Molly Brown House is open to the public from Monday through Friday from 10 a.m. to 4 p.m.; guided tours are conducted. The Victorian cutting garden is sponsored by Historic Denver.

Trinidad: The Bloom House features a re-established 1890 garden. Sponsored by the State Historical Society, it is free.

CONNECTICUT

Coventry: Caprilands Herb Farm has 14 display gardens and many plants for sale. The gardens are open to the public 9 a.m. to 5 p.m. every day including Sunday and are free. Lunch by reservation only.

Farmington: Mary McCarthy Herb Garden of the Farmington Museum is located on High Street and is open weekends in the winter and more often during the summer. The garden contains many cooking herbs and is sponsored by the museum, which dates to 1660. There is an entrance fee.

Guilford: The Henry Whitfield House on Old Whitfield Street dates to 1639 and includes a formal garden with ornamental, medicinal, and cooking herbs that were commonly used in the seventeenth century. Owned and operated by the State of Connecticut, the garden is cared for by the Leetes Island Garden Club and is open without fee Wednesday through Sunday from 10 a.m. to 5 p.m., April through November.

Litchfield: Hemlock Hill Herb Farm on Hemlock Hill Road is open from May 1 through August 31, Tuesday through Saturday, from 10 a.m. to 4 p.m. The gardens are free to the public and there are herb plants for sale.

DELAWARE

Odessa: The Corbit-Sharp House in Colonial Old Town has a colonial garden that is open any time, with no admission charged. It is sponsored by Winterthur Museum.

DISTRICT OF COLUMBIA

Washington: The Bishop's Garden at the Washington Cathedral, Mount St. Albans, is open from dawn to dusk except in inclement weather; no fee. Called a "Garden for the Ages," it features very old boxwood and a Norman arch and Norman court from the twelfth century. The All Hallows Guild sponsors the garden and operates the Herb Cottage, where herb products may be purchased. Plants are available.

The Herb Society of America has designed and contributed a $250,000 herb garden to the National Arboretum. This beautiful garden has been accepted by the Department of Agriculture on behalf of the people of the United States by an act of Congress.

FLORIDA

Gainesville: The College of Pharmacy sponsors a Medicinal Plant Garden on the university campus. It features medicinal plants and herbs, is always open and free.

GEORGIA

Pine Mountain: The Callaway Gardens features a herb garden at the main entrance to their 7½-acre vegetable garden, devoted mostly to culinary herbs and espaliered fruits and scented geraniums. Railroad ties are used to make raised beds and retaining walls. The gardens are open from 7:30 a.m. to 6 p.m., and the admission fee is for all the gardens.

ILLINOIS

Glencoe: The herb garden at the new Botanic Garden of the Chicago Horticultural Society features a knot garden of great charm and simplicity. The three plots are planted with medicinal herbs, teas, culinary herbs, and plants mentioned in the Bible. The knot is surrounded by a low wattle fence. Sponsored by the society, it is open to the public.

Springfield: Lincoln's New Salem State Park includes an herb garden.

LOUISIANA

St. Martinville: The Acadian House Museum at Longfellow Evangeline State Park has a herb garden. Open from 8:30 a.m. to 4:30 p.m., the admission is free.

MAINE

Camden: Merry Gardens on Mechanic Street is open weekdays, Monday through Saturday, admission by donation. The garden features huge rosemary bushes and a large variety of labeled plants.

Rockport: Vesper Chapel has a small, pretty herb garden.

MARYLAND

Annapolis: The Slicer-Shiplap House on Pinkney Street in the waterfront area of Annapolis, under the aegis of the Four Rivers Garden Club, is a utilitarian garden, open to the public. The plan includes herbs with medicinal and culinary virtues as they were used in the 1720 period.

MASSACHUSETTS

Pittsfield: The Herb Garden at Hancock Shaker Village is a replica of a Shaker Garden, planted with the herbs the Shakers found most useful in their medicinal herb business. Two smaller gardens containing culinary herbs and dye plants are also there, planted and cared for by the Hancock Shaker Village staff. Open 9:30 a.m. to 5:00 p.m., June 1 to November 1, an admission fee is charged for entrance to the village.

Plymouth: There are many herb gardens at Plimoth Plantation. Behind each family house in the village there is an individual, fenced plot which yields vegetables as well as herbs for medicinal, aromatic, and culinary use. Depending upon the season they come, visitors see the gardens planted, tended, or harvested and also the products used in seventeenth-century fashion. There is a fee to enter the village and this includes the gardens.

Sturbridge: Old Sturbridge Village has a herb garden of medicinal and culinary herbs. The entrance fee to the village includes entrance to the garden. It is open April through October 9:30 a.m. to 5:30 p.m. and 10:00 a.m. to 4:00 p.m. the rest of the year.

MICHIGAN

Dearborn: There are two herb gardens in Greenfield Village. Our Garden of the Leavened Heart is next to Martha Mary Chapel and the other is next to Dr. Howard's Office. Mrs. Henry Ford laid the plans for the older herb garden, which is made up of heart-shaped and triangle-shaped beds to form a circle around a central sundial. Mrs. Ford chose the plants for their medicinal and culinary values. Open weekdays from 9 a.m. to 5:30 p.m. and weekends from 9 a.m. to 6 p.m., the admission charge includes a complete tour of Greenfield Village and the gardens.

MINNESOTA

Chaska: A major herb garden is maintained by the Twin Cities Herb Society at the University of Minnesota Landscape Arboretum, 3675 Arboretum Drive. It is open to the public.

A Heritage of Herbs

MISSOURI

Lake Jacomo: Missouri Town 1855, part of the Jackson County Parks system, includes family garden plots such as provided pioneer families with their basic herbal needs.

Sainte Genevieve: The Bolduc House, built about 1770, is a restored Creole house of the colonial period and features a stockade fence, frontier kitchen, and an eighteenth-century garden. Open to the public April 1 to November 1, there is an admission charge.

St. Louis: Missouri Botanical Gardens, 2315 Tower Grove Avenue, features a formal garden laid out to complement the Victorian-style country house of Henry Shaw. Sponsored by the St. Louis Herb Society, according to proposed present plans, the garden will be doubled in size and scope. Open 10 a.m. to 4 p.m., admission is $1.00 for adults.

NEW JERSEY

Gladstone: The Willowwood Arboretum has many different gardens, including a herb garden.

Morristown: In Jockey Hollow National Park, the Tempe Wick House has a kitchen garden of the revolutionary period. It is closed Mondays; no fee.

Morristown: The Schuyler-Hamilton House at 5 Olyphant Place is a Chapter House of the DAR, open Tuesday and Friday from 2 to 5 p.m. It features a small medicinal herb garden of the colonial period.

Plainfield: Cedar Brook Park on Park Avenue has a Shakespearean garden filled with plants of the sixteenth century, the herbs mentioned by Shakespeare, all labeled with the chapter and verse. Open daily, dawn to dusk.

Port Murray: Well-Sweep Herb Farm is located on Mt. Bethel Road and is open every weekday from 9 a.m. to 5 p.m. There are specimen rosemaries, including some standards in the knot garden. No admission charge.

Somerville: The Duke Gardens Foundation, privately owned Duke estate on Route 206-S, features many elegant gardens including a well-clipped colonial one, under glass. Open all year, there is an admission fee and advance reservations are required.

Sussex: Rocky Hollow Herb Farm on Lake Wallkill Road is open from April through October, in conjunction with a farm store, every day except Monday from 10 a.m. to 6 p.m. The gardens are Mediterranean style, full of savory fragrances and the soft colors of herbs. There is no admission charged except for large groups arranged by appointment.

Trenton: The William Trent House, 539 South Warren Street, features an English knot garden, a rose garden, and a herb garden. Open weekdays from 10 a.m. to 5 p.m., Sundays from 2 to 4 p.m.

Woodbridge: The Bible Gardens of Beth Israel Memorial Park, on Route 1, are open to the public daily, except Saturday, from 9 a.m. to 4:30 p.m. and closed on legal and Jewish holidays. The four gardens illustrate significant passages from the Bible and the herbs that sheltered the Israelites and provided them with food and medicines.

NEW YORK

Brooklyn: The Brooklyn Botanic Garden, 1000 Washington Avenue, has an Elizabethan knot garden and herb garden. The gardens feature over 200 different kinds of culinary, medicinal, and dye-plant herbs. They also maintain an extensive Fragrance Garden for the Blind featuring fragrant foliage, fragrant flowers, textured foliage, and "taste" foliage plants, labeled in braille. Sponsored by the Brooklyn Institute of Arts and Sciences, the gardens are free, open every day but Monday.

Ithaca: The Robinson York State Herb Garden at Cornell University, a formal herb garden with four large raised beds, was designed as a living reference library for herb study. Open to the public every day from sunup to sundown, the 75' x 125' garden is reached from Judd Falls Road. It features 800 species of herbs, including allied woody plants used in cooking, fragrance, and medicine. Worldwide

Photo, by Philip B. Mullan, courtesy of Brooklyn Botanic Garden

The Elizabethan knot garden of the Brooklyn Botanic Garden is a charming medley of shade, shrubs, and clipped plants.

sources supplied the seed. On the wall is carved "The Herb Becomes the Teacher—Men Stray After False Goals."

New York City: The New York Botanical Garden in Bronx Park includes a herb garden designed and maintained by the New York Unit of the Herb Society of America.

New York City: The Cloisters at Fort Tryon Park features a Medieval Herb Garden that shows over 250 herbs dating back to Charlemagne. Under the auspices of the Metropolitan Museum of Art.

Old Westbury: Old Westbury Gardens, 71 Old Westbury Road, include several magnificent gardens, along with an eighteenth-century herb garden sponsored by the New York Herb Society. There is an admission fee which is for all the gardens. It is open from 10 a.m. to 5 p.m., Wednesday through Sunday, May through October.

Rochester: The Garden of Fragrance on the campus of Rochester Museum and Science Center is open to the public from 9 a.m. to sunset.

Southampton: The Thomas Halsey Homestead herb garden is maintained by the Southampton Garden Club.

NORTH CAROLINA

Manteo: The Elizabethan Garden on Roanoke Island, created and maintained by the Garden Club of North Carolina as a living memorial to our first English colonists, including the Lost Colony, is unique. Built on 10½ acres, here there is a sunken garden with parterred beds and a knot garden.

OHIO

Cleveland: The Log House Herb Garden is part of the Miles School Garden Center of the Cleveland public school system, where much gardening activity is carried out by the children. It features many useful herbs plus an hexagonal thyme garden.

Photo, by Steven A. Frowine, courtesy of
Garden Center of Greater Cleveland

A view of the magnificent knot garden at the Greater Cleveland Garden Center.

Cleveland: The Western Reserve Herb Society sponsors a formal Old World garden of outstanding design. Located at the Garden Center of Greater Cleveland, 11030 East Boulevard, it is always open, with no admission charge. The garden features 13 millstones set in walks and an elaborate knot, with smaller gardens of culinary, medicinal, and dye herbs, along with old roses. There is an old stone wall, garden seats, and a watering trough.

OKLAHOMA

Tulsa: The Anne Hathaway Municipal Herb Garden in Woodward Park is located at Peoria and 21st Streets. It is a formal 50' square with a large circle of 18 beds in the middle. This is a summer garden showing all the herbs that will grow in Oklahoma's hot summers. Over 3,000 new herb plants are set out in May each year. Labeled and available for study summer through late fall, the garden is open to the public.

OREGON

Portland: The Oregon Museum of Science and Industry, 4015 S.W. Canyon Road, has a study garden where leaders take classes for instruction. Open to the public from 9 a.m. to dusk, the garden is sponsored by the Oregon Herb Society.

PENNSYLVANIA

Ephrata: The Ephrata Cloister at 632 W. Main Street features the Beissel Kitchen Garden, a garden laid out in typical German style with herbs around the perimeter and vegetables in four raised beds in the middle. It is open daily except major holidays and there is a modest admission charge.

Harrisburg: Ft. Hunter Mansion and Museum includes a herb garden and very old boxwood plantings. It is a project of the Garden Club of Harrisburg and is always open. An admission fee is charged to enter the museum, located at 5300 N. River Road.

Harrisburg: The William Penn Museum also features two herb gardens on the upper level. Both are 85' in diameter and in the form of wagon wheels. Viewable from dawn to dusk, spring through fall.

Kennett Square: Longwood Gardens has a herb garden, among others, with a large collection of distinctly labeled herbs in separate boxes. Open daily 9 a.m. to 6 p.m., there is an admission charge.

Lima: The Fragrant Garden of the John J. Tyler Arboretum is located at the Forge and Painter Residence. Open every day from 8 a.m., it is free to the public. The garden features braille labels for the blind, four terraces, two retaining walls, and a terrace of herbs. The arboretum is assisted by the Philadelphia Unit of the Herb Society of America.

Morrisville: Pennsbury Manor, the home of William Penn, a seventeenth-century manor house, has a recreated herb garden complete with its dipping well. Administered by the Pennsylvania Historical and Museum Commission, the house is open daily, and there is a fee. The gardens include many shrubs and trees indigenous to the province, supplemented by those from England. The gardens are extensive and formal, with a large herb and vegetable garden, important to the seventeenth-century household.

Philadelphia: John Bartram's Garden, a restoration of America's first arboretum, at 54th Street and Elmwood Avenue, includes the herbs and native plants that Bartram discovered in his early travels through the "new green world." Open from 10 a.m. to 4 p.m., the garden is a Garden Club Federation of Pennsylvania project. Donations are accepted and tours can be arranged.

Philadelphia: The Drug Plant and Herb Garden of the Morris Arboretum (University of Pennsylvania) is located at 9414 Meadowbrook Avenue in Chestnut Hill. Open 9 a.m. to 5 p.m. every day, there is no admission. It features a collection of plants used for medical purposes, including many tropical species that are overwintered in the greenhouse. It is sponsored by the Morris Arboretum and The Garden Club of America.

Philadelphia: The "physick garden" of the Pennsylvania Hospital is located on the Pine Street lawn of the hospital, near 9th Street. Pennsylvania Hospital, founded by Benjamin Franklin, is the nation's first, dating from 1751. This newly created authentic eighteenth-century herb garden completes this national landmark and is open to visitors weekdays, 8:30 a.m. to 5 p.m., with no admission charge. The garden is one of several Bicentennial projects of the Philadelphia Committee of The Garden Club of America.

Pittsburgh: Old Economy Village was settled in 1804 and features a dye and medicinal herb garden. Go west to Ambridge and watch for signs. Open year round. All the herb gardens in the Pittsburgh area are sponsored by the Western Pennsylvania Unit of the Herb Society of America.

Pittsburgh: The Pioneer Woman's Yarb Patch at Settler's Cabin Regional Park, part of the Allegheny County Park system, is located in southwest Pittsburgh.

Pittsburgh: Round Hill Regional Park, on Round Hill Road at Elizabeth, is open year round. Over forty wood-edged square beds group the herbs appropriately. There is a drying shed, a large vegetable garden, and native plants which have herbal uses.

Pittsburgh: Winchester-Thurston School in the Shadyside section is a garden of colonial design with plants of international background to illustrate botany, history, literature, and horticulture, designed to teach "the heritage of knowledge." Since the students use the garden, it is suggested that the public visit after school hours or on weekends.

York: Historic Plough Tavern and Gates House, circa 1740, has a small garden of all medicinal plants. Open every day from 10 a.m. to 4 p.m. There is a charge only to see the houses.

RHODE ISLAND

Pawtucket: There is a Garden of Dye and Textile Plants at Old Slater Museum.

SOUTH CAROLINA

Charleston: There are herb gardens at Charles Towne Landing on Highway 171 and at The Heyward Washington House, 87 Church Street, Charleston.

Roebuck: The Walnut Grove Plantation features a herb garden.

SOUTH DAKOTA

Brookings: The McCrory Gardens of South Dakota State University are open daily in the summer with no admission charge. The gardens feature over 350 annual flowers, including herbs and more than 650 clones of perennial flowering plants.

UTAH

Salt Lake City: The herb garden on the campus of the University of Utah is open to the public.

VIRGINIA

Mt. Vernon: The Kitchen Garden of General Washington's home at Mt. Vernon is restored within the original enclosing walls in a manner true to the period. It features espaliered fruit trees, many vegetables, and all the herbs found necessary to a colonial household. Sponsored by the Mt. Vernon Ladies' Association, it is open every day of the year and there is a fee which covers entrance to the entire plantation and house. Seeds from the garden are available at the gift shop.

Williamsburg: John Blair Gardens on Duke of Gloucester Street is a formal garden arrangement with beds planted in various herbs. Visitors are welcome to stroll the garden, sponsored by Colonial Williamsburg Foundation, at any time.

Williamsburg: Wythe House on the Palace Green has herbs planted in rows with name tags. Although general admission is charged to the restoration at Colonial Williamsburg, people may walk in the garden from 9 a.m. to 5 p.m. daily.

WASHINGTON

Olympia: The Pioneer Herb Garden of the Washington State Capitol Museum is a collection of over fifty types of herbs which could have been brought west by the settlers for use as food or medicine. Sponsored by the Associates of the Museum, a volunteer group, the garden is open to the public every day but Mondays, at no charge.

WISCONSIN

Bayside: Schlitz Audubon Park has a new herb garden, donated by the Green Tree Garden Club. It consists of native American herbs.

Hales Corners: The Boerner Botanical Gardens in Whitnall Park, 5879 S. 92nd Street, features a herb garden that contains both common and unusual culinary, medicinal, and scented herbs. The plants are arranged in a distinctive, semiformal manner in a formal setting. Of special interest is the "Salad Bowl," a bed designed to show off the decorative qualities of vegetables. The gardens are open from 8 a.m. to sunset daily during the growing season from April through October. There are no parking or admission charges.

Garden Herbs at a Glance

ALPINE STRAWBERRY *(Fragaria semperflorens)*

Life-style: Perennial, 1'.
How to Plant: Seeds only, in early spring. Or divide old clumps.
Where and When: Traditional edging for herb gardens; full sun; good drainage.
Harvest: Pick the berries daily.
Preservation: Freeze them or use as available.
Brief Description: Nonspreading strawberry plant; constantly in fruit, bud, and flower; extremely decorative.
Special Notes: A long producing season, June through November; very sweet berries.
Uses: As a garnish, in fruit cup, cereal, jams, punch.

ANGELICA *(Angelica archangelica)*

Life-style: Biennial, 3' to 5'.
How to Plant: Seeds planted when fresh (self-sows).

Where and When: August or after freezing the seeds; in semi-shade.

Harvest: Leaves in May; seeds in July; stalks anytime available; roots in fall.

Preservation: Stalks must be candies; leaves may be dried.

Brief Description: Very tall, to 6'; large leaves, handsome chartreuse flowers, and seed heads.

Special Notes: Will self-sow where it wants to grow; a striking addition to the herb garden.

Uses: The stalks as a confection; leaves and roots medicinally; a powerful protective herb.

ANISE *(Pimpinella anisum)*

Life-style: Annual, sometimes biennial, 1'.

How to Plant: From seeds only.

Where and When: Outdoors in spring where you want it to grow, in sun or mild shade.

Harvest: Leaves anytime; seeds when ripe.

Preservation: Dry leaves or seeds thoroughly and store in dark bottles.

Brief Description: Delicate plant, quietly attractive pale green.

Special Notes: Slightly licorice flavor and, like licorice, very sweet.

Uses: Leaves or seeds with fish, shrimp, and crab; fruits, salads, and in tea; liquors, candies, cookies, and bread.

BASIL *(Ocimum basilicum* var.)

Life-style: Annual, 1' to 3'.

How to Plant: From seeds, 3 to 5 days' germination.

Where and When: Outdoors in full sun; front border, 1' apart; after danger of frost; also near tomatoes.

Harvest: Pluck leaves as needed as soon as you can; later cut sprays.

Preservation: Hang to dry in a dark place; or freeze.

Brief Description: Attractive plant in all varieties, especially the dark-red varieties; highly aromatic.

Special Notes: A good houseplant; one pot won't be enough if you like basil.

Basil

Uses: In spaghetti and all Italian dishes; in butters and vinegars; also soups, stews, and salads; grow near patios to repel flies.

BAY LAUREL *(Laurus nobilis)*

Life-style: Perennial, not hardy where winters are severe; a shrub.

How to Plant: Seeds, cuttings, or buy a plant.

Where and When: In a pot for mobility to bring indoors or as a garden feature.

Harvest: Pick the glossy green evergreen leaves as needed, one by one.

Preservation: Lay out in dry dark place to dry thoroughly and store.

Brief Description: Handsome plant when small; magnificent when full-grown in a tub.

Special Notes: Excellent houseplant when kept not too hot or damp.

Uses: A leaf is traditional in bouquet garni; add to all stews; repels weevils in pasta, rice, all starchy foods.

BORAGE *(Borago officinalis)*

Life-style: Annual, 3'.

How to Plant: Best grown from seeds.

Where and When: Sow seeds in sun and after that they will come up in strange places, where they want to, spring and fall.

Harvest: Cut leaves and flowers as needed and available.

Preservation: Leaves can be dried by hanging; Preserved in vinegar; press the pretty blue flowers.

Brief Description: A tall coarse-leaved annual that tastes of cucumber; it has brilliant blue star-shaped flowers.

Special Notes: Allow it to self-sow and you will always have borage "for courage"—frequently two crops a year.

Uses: The leaves in salads; the flowers in wine; also candied and as a garnish.

BURNET *(Sanguisorba minor)*

Life-style: Perennial, 1'.

How to Plant: Seeds only.

Where and When: In open sunny front borders, kitchen gardens; spring or fall.

Harvest: Cut and use the leaves all year.

Preservation: Best used fresh or frozen.

Brief Description: Compound leaflets form a rosette crown plant, reddish-brown flowers in late May-June.

Special Notes: Very pretty leaves with a pronounced cucumber flavor; also suitable for pressed flower pictures.

Uses: Salads, dips, with cheese, butter, and in vinegars.

CALENDULA *(Calendula officinalis)*

Life-style: Self-sowing annual, to 1'.

How to Plant: From seeds.

Where and When: On the snow or early in spring; in full sun.

Harvest: The blossoms, all summer.

Preservation: Air-dry the flowers and store in dark jars.

Brief Description: A "flower of the sun" grown for its single bright-orange daisylike flowers; very old-fashioned.

Special Notes: Was an important crop once, now colorful in any garden. IMPORTANT: also called Pot Marigold.

Uses: Petals in cookery, wine, confections, and potpourri; a first-aid plant; also for cosmetics; as a tea.

CAMOMILE, ROMAN *(Anthemis nobilis)*

Life-style: Sometimes perennial, to 1'.

How to Plant: Grow it from its very fine seeds.

Camomile

Where and When: In open areas and full sun.

Harvest: The daisylike flowers as available.

Preservation: Spread on screens to dry before storing.

Brief Description: Perennial, if climate suits; sometimes self-sows.

Special Notes: Easy to grow, if you keep the flower heads picked to assure a continuous crop.

Uses: Tea; cosmetics; insect repellent; hair rinse; and as a lawn, where it grows easily.

CARAWAY *(Carum carvi)*

Life-style: Biennial, to 3'.

How to Plant: Seeds only.

Where and When: Plant in spring, sunshine, good drainage, 10" apart.

Harvest: Gather the mature seed heads in the second year.

Preservation: Cut seed heads into a bag before they are completely ripened and they will be easier to dry, process, and store.

Brief Description: Carrot-top foliage in a rosette; ferny attractive plant until it goes to seed.

Special Notes: The foliage may be added to bouquets (or salads); the seeds have a stronger flavor than anise.

Uses: Seeds whole in bread, especially rye; cookies, cakes; in liquor (kümmel); in sauerkraut, pork, liver, beets.

CATNIP *(Nepeta cataria)*

Life-style: Perennial, from 1' to 3'.

How to Plant: Seeds or root divisions.

Where and When: Plant in sunny spot, early spring, tolerates poor soil.

Harvest: Cut the stems from early June on.

Preservation: Hang to dry; crumble the leaves off the stems and store out of light.

Brief Description: Gray-leaved foliage plants with strong minty fragrance; the wild catnip is tall, robust.

Special Notes: "If you set it cats will eat it; if you sow it, cats won't know it" — or so they say. *Nepeta mussini* is first catnip to bloom in spring in our garden.

Uses: As a tea, best iced; a tonic for kitty; a pungent mint.

CHERVIL *(Anthriscus cerefolium)*

Life-style: Short-lived annual, 1'.

How to Plant: Seeds only.

Where and When: Indoors in March or outside in spring; good drainage; partial shade.

Harvest: Gather the leaves to use fresh or dry the surplus.

Preservation: Dry on wire screens and store in dark jars.

Brief Description: Lacy-leaved delicate plant much admired in the shady garden.

Special Notes: A gourmet herb with a mild anise flavor; very pretty in pressed herb pictures; sometimes referred to as French parsley.

Uses: Just as parsley; sauces, salads, soups, and "fines herbes."

CHIVES *(Allium schoenoprasum)*

Life-style: Perennial, 1½'.

How to Plant: Seeds or divide well-established clumps.

Where and When: Full sun; good drainage is essential; plant in borders, as an edging plant or in patio pots.

Harvest: Cut the onion-flavored tops by the inch; keep them clipped for health.

Preservation: Use fresh and freeze the rest.

Brief Description: Small clumps of onionlike plants; pretty purple flowers very early in spring; dormant during winter months.

Chives

Special Notes: Easy to grow; delicious to use; can be grown in pots on sunny window sill.

Uses: A superb seasoning in dips, cottage cheese, potatoes; garnishes, vinegar, and butters.

CLARY SAGE *(Salvia sclarea)*

Life-style: Biennial, to 3'.

How to Plant: A crown plant, it must be grown from seeds.

Where and When: Early in spring, 1' apart; very good drainage, rich loam, and a place in the sun.

Harvest: The leaves.

Preservation: Usually used fresh in cookery, the leaves may be dried on screens and used in potpourri.

Brief Description: Large felted heart-shaped leaves form a magnificent plant, especially eye-catching when the flower spikes are in bloom.

Special Notes: Popular in the Middle Ages; grow clary whether you use it or not—at least once.

Uses: The leaves flavor punch, omelettes, teas, and pastries; sachets.

COMFREY *(Symphytum officinale)*

Life-style: Strong perennial, to 5' or more.

How to Plant: Seeds, root cuttings, or buy plants.

Where and When: In early spring; against fences or as background; sun or fringes of shade; will tolerate moisture and clay.

Harvest: Cut back to 3" when leaves are 3' to 5' tall.

Preservation: Hang leaves in bunches or dry in oven at 150° for ½ hour.

Brief Description: Tall growing with coarse rough green leaves; flowers if not cut back.

Special Notes: Keep comfrey cut back or it will self-sow and take over.

Uses: As a green vegetable; a tea, poultice; animal feed; valuable medicinal plant; also as green manure, compost, or mulch.

CORIANDER *(Coriandrum sativum)*

Life-style: Annual, to 3'.

How to Plant: Seeds only in early spring (or in pots during winter for *cilantro.*)

Where and When: In full sun, combined with anise seeds for best results.

Harvest: Leaves, fresh or dried; seeds when mature, late summer.

Preservation: Hang to dry the leaves; air-dry the seeds; store either in tight jars.

Brief Description: Sometimes rank-growing with strong-smelling leaves.

Special Notes: Two herbs from the same seed packet — the seeds and the leaves *(cilantro)*, which taste entirely different.

Uses: Leaves in Mexican or Indian cookery; seeds in cakes, cookies, curry, and gingerbread.

COSTMARY *(Chrysanthemum balsamita)*

Life-style: Perennial, 2' to 3'.

How to Plant: Root divisions taken in spring; divide every third year; rarely from seed.

Where and When: At least 1' apart and 1' from other plants, resents crowding; loves sun, good soil, and excellent drainage.

Harvest: Cut back before blooming; pick any leaves any time and use fresh or dried.

Preservation: Hang to dry or press the fragrant leaves flat between pages of a magazine.

Brief Description: Tall when in bloom; spear-shaped leaves, pale green, and strongly minty.

Special Notes: Likes to grow free of weeds but weeding is a fragrant task; sometimes winter-kills.

Uses: In ground meat; as a tea; to flavor drinks; Bible bookmarks, from whence it takes its common name Bibleleaf.

DILL *(Anethum graveolens)*

Life-style: Annual with a short season, to 3' or 4'.

How to Plant: Only from seeds; germinates quickly, indoors or out; sow on the snow for an early crop.

Where and When: Spring, then again in July; full sun.

Harvest: A quick crop; cut the leaves as needed; the seeds when plump and still green.

Preservation: Hang the leaves to dry; cut the seed heads into a bag and allow to dry brown; store in dark bottle.

Brief Description: Tall with feathery foliage, flowers in umbels quickly turn to seed heads; the green leaves are called dill weed.

Special Notes: Will self-sow in same area for several years if allowed to go to seed.

Uses: Seeds and stalks in pickles; green leaves (dill weed) in salads or on cottage cheese; as a sedative tea.

Dill

FENNEL *(Foeniculum vulgare)*

Life-style: Hardy annual, 3' to 5'.

How to Plant: Best from seed where it is to grow.

Where and When: In full sun as background.

Harvest: Cut the leaves anytime; the seeds are harvested when ripe.

Preservation: Air-dry seeds on fine-mesh screens; store in dark.

Brief Description: Tall ferny-leaved growth, handsome in the garden especially when in seed.

Special Notes: "Eat fennel and grow thin," said the ancient herbalists. The seeds are a natural curb to appetite.

Uses: Indispensable to fish; also curry, pork, apple dishes, and as a tea; anise-flavored.

GARLIC *(Allium sativum)*

Life-style: Perennial, 2'.

How to Plant: Buy it at the grocery; then divide the bulb into its natural segments and plant the cloves, pointed end up.

Where and When: Full sun; herb or vegetable patch; plant in fall or very early spring.

Harvest: Harvest in late summer, when the tops begin to dry, by digging the bulbs.

Preservation: Braid the tops and hang to dry; keep dry during storage.

Brief Description: Tall straplike foliage, sometimes floppy, with typical Allium flowering stalks in June-July.

Special Notes: Always replant a few bulbs (cloves) for the next year immediately after digging and assure a perpetual crop.

Uses: There is little not improved by a suggestion of garlic; salads, spaghetti, soups; also medicinal.

GERANIUMS, SCENTED *(Pelargonium* var.)

Life-style: Tender perennials, in all sizes.

How to Plant: Buy plants where available locally or through mail; propagate by cuttings.

Where and When: Best of the herbs for pot culture; grow in sunny window sill or plant in garden for the summer.

Harvest: Cut them back to your preference, gathering all the leaves you can.

Preservation: Hang stems in bunches or dry leaves on screens in a dark dry place.

Brief Description: Many leaf forms and variations in plant characteristics add interest to the herb garden, usually as specimen plants; fragrances: lemon, rose, ginger, nutmeg, apple, spice, peppermint, and others.

Special Notes: Grown for their fragrant leaves not their flowers, which are a sometime thing; edible.

Uses: Potpourris and sachets; sugars; jellies; desserts; drinks; bouquets.

GERMANDER *(Teucrium chamaedrys)*

Life-style: Perennial, 1'.

How to Plant: Root divisions, rooted cuttings, or layers.

Where and When: Average soil, full sun; along edges as part of the herb garden pattern.

Harvest: Cut the flowers for bouquets.

Preservation: Loveliest when fresh; dry by hanging if you wish.

Brief Description: When clipped, it is beautiful 12 months of the year with glossy evergreen leaves; lavender flowers in midsummer.

Special Notes: Grow it unclipped as a bee herb.

Uses: In knot gardens and other patterns; to flavor honey; medicinal (bitter).

Germander

HOP *(Humulus lupulus)*

Life-style: Strong perennial vine.

How to Plant: Seeds in fall or refrigerate 6 weeks before sowing; buy plants.

Where and When: In sun against a fence or trellis, preferably in fall.

Harvest: Pick the strobiles or cones in fall.

Preservation: Dry on screens; then pack away in tight tins.

Brief Description: A vigorous grower; male and female needed to produce seed heads, which are also pretty in dried arrangements.

Special Notes: Sometimes hard to restrain; frequently found growing wild around old foundations.

Uses: In bread, beer; the tea for insomnia; also snooze pillows; excellent for the hair.

HOREHOUND *(Marrubium vulgare)*

Life-style: Perennial, 2'.

How to Plant: Seeds or cuttings or plants.

Where and When: On sunny slopes; requires good drainage and enjoys humidity; sandy soil, enriched.

Harvest: The leaves and flower stalks.

Preservation: Hang to dry.

Brief Description: Silvery-white hoary leaves are pungent; beautiful plant.

Special Notes: Needs to be replanted every 2 to 3 years in our garden.

Uses: A tea for coughs and colds; candy, cough drops.

HORSERADISH *(Armoracia lapathifolia)*

Life-style: Perennial, 3'.

How to Plant: Root cuttings or divisions.

Where and When: Early spring in an open sunny place; good in the vegetable garden; in friable soil.

Harvest: The root from October on through spring.

Preservation: Dig and grate as needed; preserved in vinegar; store roots in cold cellar until needed.

Brief Description: Becomes a large clump of tall rank-growing leaves; common to old farms; sometimes found wild.

Special Notes: Can be dug and stored in damp sawdust through winter to grate and use fresh; pieces of root will grow new plants.

Uses: A condiment; an aid to digestion; flavor to meat, especially beef and smoked ham.

HYSSOP *(Hyssopus officinalis)*

Life-style: Perennial, 2'.

How to Plant: Seeds or cuttings or by layering.

Where and When: Full sun in the herb garden, in a rockery, or as an accent plant; also as low hedging; in spring.

Harvest: The flowers for bouquets; cut the stalks to shape the plant, rarely used today.

Preservation: Hang to dry; or press the lovely flowers.

Brief Description: A dense evergreen when kept clipped, loose open form when grown naturally.

Special Notes: A "Bible" herb gathered during Lenten season and used symbolically. *(Origanum maru is the true hyssop of the Bible.)*

Uses: One of the bitter herbs rarely in use today except as an attractive garden plant.

Hyssop

LAVENDER *(Lavandula officinalis var.)*

Life-style: Perennial; sometimes needs renewal, 1' to 3'.

How to Plant: Seeds; cuttings; root divisions; purchased plants.

Where and When: In spring, full sun, well-limed soil, with some protection from wind.

Harvest: Cut back in early spring; harvest right before buds open for strongest fragrance, or when necessary.

Preservation: Hang the flowers to dry; the leaves are dried in bunches or on screens.

Brief Description: Can be clipped to 1' height or will spread 3' x 3' if site is suitable; a most attractive gray-leaved plant.

Lavender

Special Notes: Lavender frequently winter-kills in northern latitudes; plant against rocks, buildings, or shrubbery to give protection against high winds.

Uses: Grown for fragrance; sometimes medicinal and culinary; sachets, bath waters, sweet bags, and potpourri.

LEMON BALM *(Melissa officinalis)*

Life-style: Perennial, 1½′.

How to Plant: Seeds; root divisions.

Where and When: Sun or semishade; in spring.

Harvest: Before it flowers in June; again in late summer.

Preservation: Hang in loose bunches in dark dry place; strip dried leaves into tight containers.

Brief Description: Chartreuse foliage has strong lemon scent; unobtrusive flower spikes produce hundreds of unwanted seedlings. Beware!

Special Notes: Wonderfully easy herb to grow and very useful; plant in pots to bring indoors in January as a houseplant.

Balm

Uses: Tea, lemon balm alone, or a few leaves in regular tea; in fish, with fruit, salads, herb sugars, all drinks, and as a garnish.

LEMON VERBENA *(Lippia citriodora)*

Life-style: Tender perennial, to 6'.
How to Plant: Rooted woody cuttings taken anytime; or plants.
Where and When: In pots for house culture; prefers a sunny cool window; plant in garden in spring.
Harvest. The leaves, every one that falls, and all clippings.
Preservation: Dry leaves on screens until crisp to touch; store in tight tins.
Brief Description: Handsome South American shrub with pale-green leaves, exceedingly lemony fragrance; after a few years it is almost treelike and becomes a tub plant.
Special Notes: Needs a rest period every year; when the leaves drop, move out of the sun and water only when dry; collect the dropped leaves.
Uses: Lemon sachets, potpourris; sugars, punch, and tea; bouquets.

LOVAGE *(Levisticum officinale)*

Life-style: Perennial, 3' to 6'.
How to Plant: Plants, root divisions, or seeds.
Where and When: Spring in sunny background positions; demands good drainage, limed soil, some bonemeal.

Harvest: Cut the tops before it flowers; the root may be dug in fall.

Preservation: Hang in bunches or dry quickly in slow oven (150°) for ½ hour until crisp.

Brief Description: Tall strong perennial, a great addition to any garden; flowers in large umbels.

Special Notes: Looks, smells, and tastes like celery, except that it is both stronger and larger; easy to grow.

Uses: Soups, stews, dips, or salads; also love baths; root used medicinally; in teas; use the leaves, discard the stalks.

MARJORAM *(Origanum vulgare)*

Life-style: Perennial, sometimes tender, 1½ '.

How to Plant: Seeds; cuttings; root divisions.

Where and When: In sunny area; on wasteland and banks; spring only; also in pots for patio or window sill.

Harvest: Cut the tops as often as you like, before flowering.

Preservation: Hang to dry; or preserve in vinegars; also by freezing.

Brief Description: If not cut back, this rampant grower prostrates itself all over the garden; lovely pinky-purple flowers, small dark-green leaves.

Special Notes: Many kinds of marjoram/oregano; when you find the one you like, propagate it by cuttings and winter over indoors or outside with protection from Washington south.

Uses: All Mediterranean dishes; potpourri; Advent wreaths; salads, medicinal (teas and pillows for asthma).

Marjoram

MINT *(Mentha* var.)

Life-style: Perennial, 1' to 2'.

How to Plant: Easiest from root divisions; seeds.

Where and When: Sun; tolerates semishade and dampness.

Harvest: The tops when 1' tall; cut back vigorously.

Preservation: Air-dry by hanging; or in a warm oven; large quantities can be done on sheets in a dark dry room.

Brief Description: Vigorously spreading, strongly scented perennial of many varieties; almost all may be characterized as weedy.

Special Notes: Keep it out of a patterned herb garden or plant in a tub or contained area; it is the most popular of all the herbs despite its invasiveness.

Uses: Teas, hot or iced; sugar; cookies; as a garnish; in juleps and other drinks; use every bit of it.

MONARDA *(Monarda didyma)*

Life-style: Perennial, 2' to 3'.

How to Plant: Best from division of clumps, in spring; sometimes from seed.

Where and When: In sunny areas or the fringes of shade; as early in spring as possible; will grow in wet spots.

Harvest: The tops when in flower or the leaves anytime.

Preservation: Hang to dry the flowers; leaves air-dry easily.

Brief Description: An American native, beautiful in flower, fields of it can be found in New York and New England; red through shades of purple.

Special Notes: A bee herb (sometimes called bee balm); will spread like mint if it's happy; the dried seedpods are lovely in arrangements.

Uses: As a tea, the leaves must be boiled; or add a few flowers to regular tea for flavor; in the bee garden.

MUSTARD *(Brassica* var.*)*

Life-style: Annual, 1'.
How to Plant: Seeds.
Where and When: In spring in rows in the herb or vegetable garden; or in pots for quick greens.
Harvest: The leaves when young for pungent seasoning; the seeds when ripe.
Preservation: The leaves are eaten fresh; gather every seed or you'll have a field of mustard; store in opaque jars.
Brief Description: A weedy-looking plant if allowed to go to seed; bright-yellow flowers brighten the landscape in May.
Special Notes. Thank the earliest settlers for our fields of mustard; except for the peppery greens, buy the seeds; Oriental mustard seeds are very hot.
Uses: The seeds for pepper cabbage, pickles, salads; as sprouts; also ground in mustards; and for plasters.

NASTURTIUM *(Tropaeolum majus)*

Life-style: Annual, 1'.
How to Plant: From seeds; root cuttings in water to obtain more plants.
Where and When: In May, in full sun; as an edging; plant where plants are to remain.
Harvest: Leaves and flowers and seeds—all used as seasoning.
Preservation: Use fresh; seeds in vinegar.
Brief Description: Stunning, colorful addition to the herb garden; there's a climbing variety.
Special Notes: Leaves are peppery, very much like watercress; seedpods are pungent, like capers.
Uses: In sandwiches, salads, soups, and as a colorful garnish.

ONIONS *(Allium* var.*)*

Life-style: Many kinds, mostly biennial to 18".
How to Plant: From sets (small bulbs in early spring); seeds.

Where and When: In well-drained rich soil; full sun; give fertilizer; usually planted in the vegetable garden in early spring.

Harvest: Ready in 120 days from planting sets.

Preservation: Store in dry place after tops die back and are cut off 1″ above bulb.

Brief Description: Grown for its succulent bulbs, tops can be cut at any time for seasoning or young onions pulled as spring scallions.

Special Notes: Try top-setting onions in the herb garden for interest, conversation, and food value.

Uses: As a vegetable; in soups, almost everything; also medicinally.

PARSLEY *(Petroselinum* var.)

Life-style: Biennial, to 1′.

How to Plant: Seeds for all varieties; soak them overnight for faster germination (2 to 3 weeks).

Where and When: Plant seeds indoors in March; outdoors in April or August; full sun; as an edging.

Harvest: Cut the outer green leaves anytime.

Preservation: Freeze snippets; alternate salt and parsley in a jar; oven-dry at 150° until chip dry.

Brief Description: Low-growing edging plant with dark-green leaves, sometimes curled; suitable for indoor pot culture in full sun.

Special Notes: Plant plain parsley for greater flavor; curled parsley for garnishes.

Uses: Use it generously in all soups, salads, sauces; in butters, vinegars, and salts.

PENNYROYAL AMERICAN *(Hedeoma pulegioides)*

Life-style: Annual, 12″.

How to Plant: From seeds in spring; frequently self-sows.

Where and When: Sun to semishade; likes dry places.

Harvest: Cut before flowering in June.

Preservation: Hang in bunches in dark dry place.

Brief Description: Upright small-leaved mint with pretty lavender spikes when in bloom.

Special Notes: Native herb and common; easy to grow once started; best gathered in the wild.

Uses: Tea; insect repellent; strewing herb; purifies water.

PENNYROYAL ENGLISH *(Mentha pulegium)*

Life-style: Sometimes perennial, 6".

How to Plant: From seeds in spring; or rooted cuttings.

Where and When: Sun to semishade; tolerates moist spots; low-growing edging plant.

Harvest: The green leaves, as any mint.

Preservation: Spread on screen to dry.

Brief Description: Prostrate matlike growth makes a good patch.

Special Notes: Strong flavor; perennial only in mild climates.

Uses: Same as American pennyroyal.

POPPY *(Papaver somniferum)*

Life-style: Annual, 1'.

How to Plant: Seeds only.

Where and When: In spring, or on the snow, where they are to grow; full sun.

Harvest: The ripened seedpods are collected for the seeds.

Preservation: Store dried seeds in tightly stoppered bottles.

Brief Description: Elegant in bloom, one of the showier herbs; *P. somniferum* is the poppy seed of commerce; flowers are pink through shades of lavender and gray.

Special Notes: Opium is obtained from the unripened seedpods; ALL poppy seeds are edible.

Uses: To top rolls, bread, cookies, and in cakes; noodles, dips, dressings.

ROSE *(Rosa var.)*

Life-style: Strong perennial, in all sizes; miniature to shrubs.

How to Plant: Plants from a specialist; or cuttings.

Where and When: In background, against trellis or fence; full sun; well-drained rich soil; early spring or late fall.

Harvest: Petals in June; hips (seedpods) after frost.

Preservation: Air-dry petals or hips on screens before storing.

Brief Description: Mostly tall-growing vigorous shrubs (old-fashioned); fragrant flowers in June, sometimes again later.

Special Notes: The old-fashioned roses are especially usable as herbs but substitute modern hybrids if you like; do not use poisonous sprays.

Uses: Petals in cookery, wine, confections, and potpourri; hips in tea, soup, and jellies.

ROSEMARY *(Rosmarinus officinalis)*

Life-style: Tender perennial, from 1' to 6'.

How to Plant: Seeds; cuttings; plants.

Where and When: Plant in pots anytime; outdoors after danger of frost; full sun; limed soil; also well drained.

Harvest: The leaves, singly or tips or stems, depending upon the size of your plant.

Preservation: Hang to dry or use fresh from the window sill.

Brief Description: Needlelike leaves on upright, shrubby plants; blue flowers in midwinter; pine-scented.

Special Notes: As a houseplant, rosemary likes it sunny and cool, resents fertilizers; mist plant constantly for humidity.

Uses: Beef, lamb, pork; soups and salads; fish, chicken; in shampoos; medicinally; and symbolically "for remembrance."

Rosemary

RUE *(Ruta graveolens)*

Life-style: Perennial, 2'.

How to Plant: Seeds; or cuttings only for variety "Blue Beauty."

Where and When: Spring in full sun, although a small amount of shade is tolerated; well-drained soil.

Harvest: Cut when large enough, as desired.

Preservation: Hang to dry; press leaves; or in vinegar (strong).

Brief Description: Outstanding in the garden when sun illuminates the blue leaves; insignificant yellowish flowers.

Special Notes: Bitter herb of the Early Church; ancient "herb of grace" oil in the leaves can cause a rash in hot summer; be careful picking or weeding around rue.

Uses: Use sparingly in cookery; insect repellent; strewing herb; medicinal.

SAFFRON *(Crocus sativus)*

Life-style: Bulb, perennial, 6" to 8".

How to Plant: Buy bulbs in the fall; seeds on the market are usually safflower or "false saffron."

Where and When: Plant in full sun in front of border; mark the spot.

Harvest: Collect the orange stigmas in fall while in bloom.

Preservation: Spread stigmas on clean white paper to dry (3 days); store in tight jars.

Brief Description: Looks and grows like a crocus, flowering in fall; lavender flowers.

Special Notes: It takes several years to establish a bed of saffron; can be divided and extended.

Uses: Chicken, seafood, rice, eggs, breads, Spanish cookery; medicinal; dye plant.

SAGE *(Salvia officinalis)*

Life-style: Perennial, to 3'.

How to Plant: Seeds, cuttings, layers, or plants.

Where and When: Seeds indoors in late winter; plant in full sun in early spring; requires good drainage.

Harvest: The longest stems anytime from June on; leaves all year round.

Preservation: Hang to dry; preserve the leaves whole, until needed, in dark containers.

Brief Description: Textured gray-leaved herb to 3' high and wide; very handsome; also other varieties such as golden, purple, tri-colored, all attractive and edible.

Special Notes: An easy plant to grow; lasts well; replace when harvests lessen.

Uses: Tea; seasoning for turkey stuffing; in stewed tomatoes or string beans; in butter; medicinal.

SANTOLINA *(Santolina var.)*

Life-style: Perennial, 1'.

How to Plant: From cuttings; sometimes seeds are available; plants.

Where and When: In spring, in full sun; good drainage; superb rock garden plant.

Harvest: Trim to maintain at size desired all during growing season.

Preservation: Spread on screens to dry.

Brief Description: Small-leaved shrubby herb, usually gray (also one common green variety); especially useful in borders.

Special Notes: Pungent fragrance; handsome garden plant all year through.

Uses: Insect repellent; moth chasers; herb wreaths; to create knot patterns in herb gardens.

Santolina

SAVORY, SUMMER *(Satureja hortensis)*

Life-style. Annual, 1'.

How to Plant: Seeds.

Where and When: Spring in the garden; indoors anytime; with beans in the vegetable garden.

Harvest: Cut tops in June or as needed.

Preservation: Freeze; hang in bunches; or in butter.

Brief Description. Summer savory is "the bean herb"—plant it with beans; eat it with beans.

Special Notes: A quick-crop plant; cuttings sometimes root in water for winter pot plants.

Uses: In cookery with everything, especially beans, all kinds.

SAVORY, WINTER *(Satureja montana)*

Life-style: Perennial, 1'.

How to Plant: Cuttings, root divisions, or seeds.

Where and When: Spring through early summer; in full sun.

Harvest: Harvest before blooming, or anytime during the year as needed.

Preservation: Spread on screens to dry; store in tight jars.

Brief Description: Attractive dark-green small-leaved plant; lavender flowers; evergreen.

Special Notes. May be used interchangeably with above, but more robust in flavor.

Uses: A bee plant; in knot gardens; medicinally.

SORREL *(Rumex acetosa)*

Life-style: Perennial, 2' or more.

How to Plant: Seeds; root divisions.

Where and When: Early spring; full sun; as an accent or background plant.

Harvest: Start cutting the leaves in earliest spring; again in late fall.

Preservation: Use fresh when available; freeze for soups; dry by hanging.

Brief Description: Tall when in flower, which are best discouraged; the leaves are most succulent in spring.

Special Notes: An ancient herb cultivated by the Romans; highly acid.

Uses: Soups, salads; meat tenderizer; as a vegetable; sauces; in bean soup.

SOUTHERNWOOD *(Artemisia arbrotanum)*

Life-style: Perennial, subshrub, 3'.

How to Plant: Cuttings; divisions; or by layering long side shoots.

Where and When: Full sun; early spring; give it room to spread out.

Harvest: Cut back to control shape of bush at any time and harvest trimmings.

Preservation: Hang to dry.

Brief Description: A feathery gray-green woody shrub with insignificant flowers.

Special Notes: Camphorlike fragrance makes this a desirable addition to wooden chests.

Uses: Moth repellent; shampoos; bouquets; pressed flower pictures.

SWEET CICELY *(Myrrhis odorata)*

Life-style: Perennial, to 3'.

How to Plant: Seeds, in fall or as soon as ripened; in spring if refrigerated; also by root divisions.

Where and When: Shaded moist areas; 2' to 3' apart.

Harvest: Leaves and unripe seeds.

Preservation: Dry by hanging; air-dry seeds.

Brief Description: Lacy fernlike plant, as wide as high; stunning jet-black seeds.

Special Notes: Beautiful in any garden; the fresh seeds need a cold period to germinate.

Uses: Salads; potpourris; bee herb; edible root; seeds as a spice; decorative.

SWEET WOODRUFF *(Asperula odorata)*

Life-style: Perennial, 8" to 10".
How to Plant: Root divisions are best; also from seed.
Where and When: Always in shade; in spring as soon as soil can be worked.
Harvest: The flowering stems in May.
Preservation: Dry in oven at 150° for 30 minutes; or air-dry.
Brief Description: Whorled bright-green leaves; starry-white flowers in May.
Special Notes: Fragrant only when dry; always used dried; a pretty ground cover for shade.
Uses: The main ingredient in "Maybowle"; also potpourris; fragrant pillows.

TANSY *(Tanacetum vulgare)*

Life-style: Perennial, 3'.
How to Plant: Seeds; root divisions of established clumps.
Where and When: Early in spring; sunny open areas; seeds may be started indoors.
Harvest: Reduce the tall stalks by half in late May or June.
Preservation: Hang to dry; crumble off the crisp leaves to save for use.
Brief Description: Ferny leaves; bright golden buttons for flowers; pungent odor; roots can be invasive; do not move or divide after the plant is full grown in midsummer.
Special Notes: Tansy ingested in excessive quantities is potentially dangerous.
Uses: Used in colonial cookery; also medicinally; best as an ant repellent, fresh or dried.

TARRAGON *(Artemisia dracunculus)*

Life-style: Perennial, 1½'.
How to Plant: NEVER from seed; take cuttings; buy only the true culinary tarragon.
Where and When: Part sun; as a border; in spring; excellent drainage required.
Harvest: Cut tops during the summer as available.

Tarragon

Preservation: Dry in dark place on screens; preserve the whole leaves fresh in vinegar; pluck dried leaves from stems and pack carefully in dark jar, crumble only as needed.

Brief Description: Small-leaved plant; not much to look at but, oh, the flavor!

Special Notes: Anise flavor is best when used fresh, especially in spring; can be grown on a sunny window sill.

Uses: A culinary herb for chicken, salads, seafood, lamb, tomatoes.

THYME *(Thymus vulgaris)*

Life-style: All varieties are perennial, 1', or less.

How to Plant: Seeds, cuttings, or plants.

Where and When: Full sun; early spring; along edges of other plantings.

Harvest: Cut back before flowering; again later in the season.

Preservation: Hang small bunches to dry; then strip the leaves and store in tightly stoppered jar.

Brief Description: Small woody herb with tiny leaves and flowers in white through red through purple.

Special Notes: Although the culinary varieties grow taller, the matlike thymes may be planted between stepping-stones where they tolerate light traffic.

Uses: In everything in moderation; fish, stews, chowders, salads, eggs; pungent when dried.

WATERCRESS *(Nasturtium officinalis)*

Life-style: Aquatic perennial; low-growing.

How to Plant: Start from seeds and transplant to edge of the stream; or root cuttings in damp sand.

Where and When: Plant cuttings or plants near the water (cold and moving) and it will naturalize itself.
Harvest: Cut the tops freely; all parts are edible.
Preservation: Perishable, best used when fresh.
Brief Description: Dark-green leaves found in many streams.
Special Notes: If you buy a bunch, root half in a glass of water and cut tops as needed.
Uses: A peppery seasoning; sandwiches; garnish for salads.

WORMWOOD *(Artemisia absinthium)*

Life-style: Perennial, to 3'.
How to Plant: Cuttings; root divisions; or seeds in spring or fall.
Where and When: In the sun and by itself; easy to grow; background plant.
Harvest: Cut the long sprays when in flower.
Preservation: Hang to dry or tie to wreath forms while fresh to make herb wreaths.
Brief Description: Silvery foliage with coarse leaf forms that dry well and are fragrant.
Special Notes: Gather every bit you can grow to use in herb crafts.
Uses: A bitter herb; medicinal; insect repellent; strewing; crafts; used to make absinthe.

YARROW *(Achillea millefolium)*

Life-style: Perennial, 1'.
How to Plant: Root divisions; also from seed.
Where and When: Open sunny well-drained areas.
Harvest: Rarely harvested today; cut and enjoy the flowers.
Preservation: The flowers may be hung and dried for winter bouquets; hang leaves to dry; or press for crafts.
Brief Description: Pretty in the garden, especially in bloom.
Special Notes: Sometimes invasive; plant it in a separate area.
Uses: Once used medicinally; now decorative.

Photo, by Gottscho-Schleisner, courtesy of Brooklyn Botanic Garden

The Fragrance Garden of the Brooklyn Botanic Garden, where the beds are elevated and the labels are in braille.

Bibliography

Angier, Bradford. *Field Guide to Edible Wild Plants*. Harrisburg: Stackpole Books, 1975.

Baker, Margaret. *Discovering the Folklore of Plants*. England: Shire Publications, 1969.

Balls, Edward K. *Early Uses of California Plants*. Los Angeles: University of California Press, 1972.

Bartram, Wm. *Travels of Wm. Bartram,* edited by Mark Van Doren. Original, 1792. New York: Dover Publications, 1928.

Beeton, Mrs. Isabella. *The Book of Household Management*. London, 1861. Reprint, New York: Farrar, Straus, and Giroux, 1968.

Beston, Henry. *Herbs and the Earth*. New York: Doubleday & Co., 1935.

Brown, Alice Cooke. *Early American Herb Recipes*. New York: Bonanza, 1966.

Brownlow, Margaret. *Herbs and the Fragrant Garden,* 2d ed. New York: McGraw-Hill Book Co., 1963.

Bullock, Mrs. Helen. *The Williamsburg Art of Cookery or Accomplish'd Gentlewoman's Companion*. Original, 1742. Reprint, Colonial Williamsburg, Va., 1966.

Bunyard, Edward A. *Old Garden Roses*. England: Country Life Ltd., 1936.

Bibliography

Campbell, Mary Mason. *Betty Crocker's Kitchen Gardens.* New York: Universal Publishing, Inc., 1971.

Clarkson, Rosetta E. *Herbs: Their Culture and Uses.* New York: The Macmillan Company, 1942.

———. *Herbs and Savory Seeds* (1939). Reprint, New York: Dover Publications, 1972.

Coats, Peter. *Flowers in History.* New York: The Viking Press, Inc., 1970.

Collin, Mary A. *Everyday Cooking with Herbs.* Garden City, N.Y.: Doubleday & Co., 1974.

Cooke, Alistair. *America.* New York: Alfred A. Knopf, Inc., 1974.

Coon, Nelson. *Using Wayside Plants for Healing.* New York: Hearthside Press, Inc., 1962.

———. *The Dictionary of Useful Plants.* Emmaus, Pa.: Rodale Press, 1974.

Culbreth, David M. R., M.D. *A Manual of Materia Medica and Pharmacology.* Philadelphia: Lea and Febiger, 1927.

Culpeper, Nicholas (1616-1654). *Culpeper's Complete Herbal: A Comprehensive Description of Nearly All Herbs with Their Medicinal Properties and Directions for Compounding the Medicines Extracted from Them.* Reprint, London: W. Foulsham & Co., Ltd.

Dutton, Joan Parry. *The Flower World of Williamsburg.* Colonial Williamsburg, Va., 1962.

Earle, Alice Morse. *Old Time Gardens.* New York: The Macmillan Company, 1901.

Fisher, Louise B. *An Eighteenth Century Garland.* Colonial Williamsburg, Va., 1951.

Fletcher, H. L. V. *Herbs.* England: Drake Publishers, 1972.

Foley, Daniel J., ed. *Herbs for Use and for Delight: An Anthology from The Herbalist.* A publication of The Herb Society of America. New York: Dover Publications, 1974.

Foster, Gertrude B. *Herbs for Every Garden.* New York: E. P. Dutton & Co., Inc., 1966.

Fox, Helen Morgenthau. *Gardening with Herbs for Flavor and Fragrance.* Reprint, New York: Dover Publications, 1970.

Freeman, Margaret B. *Herbs for the Mediaeval Household.* New York: The Metropolitan Museum of Art, 1971.

Gibbons, Euell. *Stalking the Healthful Herbs.* New York: David McKay Co., Inc., 1966.

Grieve, Mrs. M. *A Modern Herbal.* In 2 vols. London: Hafner Publishing, 1970.

Hermann, Matthias. *Herbs and Medicinal Flowers.* New York: Galahad Books, 1973.

Humphries, Pat, and Reppert, Bertha. *Potpourri: Recipes and Crafts.* Mechanicsburg, Pa.: The Rosemary House, 1973.

Bibliography

Jaques, H. E. *Plants We Eat and Wear*. Published by the author. Iowa: Mt. Pleasant, 1943.

Jones, Dorothy Bovee. *The Herb Garden*. Philadelphia, Dorrance & Co., 1972.

Keays, Mrs. Frederick Love. *Old Roses*. New York: The Macmillan Company, 1935.

Kelsey, Harlan P., and Dayton, William A. *Standardized Plant Names*. U.S. Department of Agriculture for the American Joint Committee on Horticultural Nomenclature. Harrisburg, PA.: J. Horace McFarland Co., 1942.

Koogle, J. D. *The Farmer's Own Book*. Baltimore: McCoull & Slater, 1857.

Krochmal, Connie. *A Guide to Natural Cosmetics*. New York: Quadrangle Press, 1973.

Lehner, Ernest and Johanna. *Folklore and Odysseys of Food and the Medicinal Plants*. New York: Tudor Publishing Co., 1962.

Leighton, Ann. *Early American Gardens "for Meate or Medicine."* Boston: Houghton Mifflin Co., 1970.

Levy, Juliette de Bairacli. *Herbal Handbook for Farm and Stable*. London: Faber and Faber Ltd., 1963.

Leyel, Mrs. C. F. *The Magic of Herbs*. London: Jonathan Cape, 1932.

Lust, John. *The Herb Book*. New York: Bantam Books, 1974.

McFarland, J. Horace. *Standardized Plant Names*. J. Horace McFarland Co. for the American Joint Committee on Horticultural Nomenclature. Harrisburg: Mt. Pleasant Press, 1942.

Meyer, Joseph E. *The Herbalist*. Original, 1918. Reprint, New York: Sterling Publishing Co., 1973.

Miloradovich, Milo. *The Art of Cooking with Herbs and Spices*. Garden City, N.Y.: Doubleday & Co., 1950.

Montagne, Prosper. *Larousse Gastronomique, The Encyclopedia of Food, Wine & Cookery*. New York: Crown Publishers, Inc., 1961.

Petulengro, Gipsy. *Romany Remedies and Recipes*. Reprint, Hollywood: Newcastle Publishing, 1972.

Philbrick, Helen, and Gregg, Richard. *Companion Plants and How to Use Them*. Old Greenwich, Conn.: The Devin-Adair Company, 1974.

Phipps, Frances. *Colonial Kitchens, Their Furnishings, and Their Gardens*. New York: Hawthorn Books, 1972.

Pollock, Allan. *Botanical Index to All the Medicinal Plants, Barks, Roots, Seeds and Flowers Usually Kept by Druggists*. New York: Allan Pollock, 1874.

Rohde, Eleanour Sinclair. *A Garden of Herbs* (1939). Reprint, New York: Dover Publications, 1969.

——— . *The Old English Herbals* (1922). Reprint, New York: Dover Publications, 1971.

Bibliography

Rosengarten, Frederic, Jr. *The Book of Spices*. Philadelphia: Livingston Publishing Co., 1969.

Shaeffer, Elizabeth. *Dandelion, Pokeweed, and Goosefoot*. Reading, Mass.: Young Scott Books, 1972.

Simmons, Adelma Grenier. *The Illustrated Herbal Handbook*. New York: Hawthorn Books, 1972.

Smith, Bradley. *Spain: A History in Art*. New York: Simon and Schuster, 1966.

Stimpson, George. *A Book About a Thousand Things*. New York: Harper & Bros., 1946.

Taylor, Norman, ed. *The Garden Dictionary*. Boston and New York: Houghton Mifflin Co., 1936.

Taylor, Raymond L. *Plants of Colonial Days*. Williamsburg, Va.: Printed for Colonial Williamsburg by the Dietz Press, 1952.

Thomas, Graham Stuart. *The Old Shrub Roses*. Boston: Charles T. Branford Co., 1956.

Thomas, John J. *The American Fruit Culturist*. New York: William Wood and Co., 1885.

Webster, Helen Noyes. *Herbs: How to Grow Them and How to Use Them*. Boston: Charles T. Branford Co., 1959.

Wieand, Paul R. *Folk Medicine Plants Used in the Pennsylvania Dutch Country*. Allentown, Pa.: Wieand's Pennsylvania Dutch, 1961.

Willison, George F. *Saints and Strangers*. New York: Reynal & Hitchcock, 1945.

Wright, Richardson. *The Story of Gardening*. New York: Garden City Publishing, 1938.

U.S. Dept. of Agriculture. *Drug Plants Under Cultivation*. Farmers Bulletin No. 663, Washington, D.C.: Govt. Printing Office, 1915.

(author unknown). *All You Need to Know About Herbs*. A periodical. London: Marshall Cavendish Ltd., 1973.

———. *Dye Plants and Dyeing, A Handbook*. New York: Brooklyn Botanic Gardens, 1965.

———. The "Home Queen" World's Fair Souvenir Cook Book. Philadelphia: J. W. Keeler & Co., 1893.

Index

Index

Index

Index

Index

swamp holly, 36
swamp magnolia, 42
swamp mallow, 49
swamp rose, 50
swamp squawroot, 48
sweet bay, 42
sweet cicely, 178
sweet fern, 54
sweet flag, 29
sweet herb bouquet, 72
sweet pepperbush, 54
sweet shrub, 29
sweet woodruff, 179
sweetgum, 54
sycamore, 55
symbolism of herbs, 98

tansy, 92, 95, 178
tarragon, 71, 178
teas, 117
thyme, 80, 87, 98, 179
tobacco, 38, 55, 66, 67, 91
tomato ketchup, 128
trailing arbutus, 24
tree hydrangea, 37
trillium, 55
trout, clay-jacketed, 126
trumpet vine, 55
tulip tree, 55
turkey corn, 55
turnip slaw, 127
turtlehead, 55

violet, 55, 91, 98
Virginia creeper, 56
Virginia pine, 47
virgin's bower, 31

wahoo, 56

walpole tea, 44
Washington, George, 65, 77, 80, 92, 109, 111
watercress, 179
wax myrtle, 25
weed soup, 127
white Cherokee rose, 50
white pine, 47
whortleberry, 37
wild alum, 31
wild bean, 35
wild bergamot, 87
wild cherries, 30
wild flower gardens, 22
wild garlic, 34
wild indigo, 38
wild plum, 47
wild rice, 49
Williamsburg, Va., 77, 150
willow oak, 45
winter savory, 176
winterberry, 23
wintergreen, 56, 91
wintergreen rub, 116
wisteria, 56
witch hazel, 57
woad, 61, 94-95
wormwood, 92, 180
wrinkles mixture, 114

yam, wild, 56
yarrow, 92, 180
yaupon, 57
yeast recipe, Shaker, 74
yellow lotus, 57
yellow wood, 57
Yerba Buena, 57
Yerba Santa, 57
yew, 109
yucca, 58
Yummy Apple Cake, 132

192